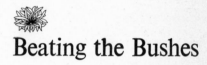

Beating the Bushes

JOHN CROWE RANSOM

Beating the Bushes

Selected Essays 1941–1970

A NEW DIRECTIONS BOOK

Some of these essays were first published in *The Kenyon Review* and are included in this collection by arrangement with Kenyon College.

Manufactured in the United States of America
First published clothbound and as New Directions Paperbook 324 in 1972
Published simultaneously in Canada by McClelland & Stewart, Ltd.

Designed by Gertrude Huston

New Directions Books are published for James Laughlin
by New Directions Publishing Corporation,
333 Sixth Avenue, New York 10014

Contents

Wanted: An Ontological Critic   1

An Address to Kenneth Burke   47

Positive and Near-Positive Aesthetics   72

Art Needs a Little Separating   80

Art Worries the Naturalists   93

Beating the Naturalists with the Stick of Drama   119

Art and the Human Economy   128

The Iconography of the Master   136

Poets and Flatworms   149

Why Critics Don't Go Mad   157

The Concrete Universal   170

Beating the Bushes

Wanted: An Ontological Critic (*1941*)

1

[A POEM DIFFERENTIATES ITSELF for us, very quickly and convincingly, from a prose discourse. We have examined some important new critics who sense this fact but do not quite offer a decisive version of what the differentia is.

It is not moralism, for moralism conducts itself very well in prose, and conducts itself all the better in pure or perfect prose. And the good critics who try to regard the poem as a moral discourse do not persuade themselves, and discuss the poem really on quite other grounds.

It is not emotionalism, sensibility, or "expression." Poetry becomes slightly disreputable when regarded as not having any special or definable content, and as identified only by its capacity for teasing some dormant affective states into some unusual activity. And it is impossible to talk definitively about the affections which are involved, so that affective criticism is highly indistinct.

Much more promising as a differentia is the kind of structure exemplified by a poem. The good critics come round to this in the end. But it is hard to say what poetry intends by its odd structure. What is the value of a structure which (a) is not so tight and precise on its logical side as a scientific or technical prose structure generally is, and (b) imports and carries along a great deal of irrelevant or foreign matter which is clearly not structural but even obstructive? This a- and b-formulation is what we inevitably come to if we take the analysis our best critics offer. We sum it up by saying that the poem is a loose logical structure with a good deal of local texture.

It is my feeling that we have in poetry a revolutionary departure from the convention of logical discourse, and that we should provide it with a bold and proportionate designation. I believe it has proved easy to work out its structural differentiation from prose. But what is the significance of this when we have got it? The structure proper is the prose of the poem, being a logical discourse of almost any kind, and dealing with almost any suitable content. The texture, likewise, seems to be of any real content that may be come upon, provided it is so free, unrestricted, and extended, that it cannot properly get into the structure. One guesses that it is an *order* of content, rather than a kind of content, that distinguishes texture from structure, and poetry from prose. At any rate, a moral content is a kind of content which has been suggested as the peculiar content of poetry, and it does not work; it is not really peculiar to poetry but perfectly available for prose. I suggest that the differentia of poetry as discourse is an ontological one. It treats an order of existence, a grade of objectivity, which cannot be treated in scientific discourse.

2

This should not prove unintelligible. We live in a world that must be distinguished from the world, or the worlds, for there are many of them, which we treat in our scientific discourses. They are its reduced, emasculated, and docile versions. Poetry intends to recover the denser and more refractory original world which we know loosely through our perceptions and memories. By this supposition it is a kind of knowledge which is radically or ontologically distinct.

2

I have failed to find a new critic with an ontological account of poetry. But I almost thought I had found a new philosopher, or aesthetician, with one. It would have been Mr. Charles W. Morris, of the University of Chicago and the *Encyclopedia of Unified Science.* I had his name at first in the title at the top of this paper. But I could not study his aesthetic achievement very long without seeing that, though he got to the point where one further step would have taken him into an ontological conception of poetry, he held back and did not take that step; either as if he lacked the speculative curiosity to go further, or as if the prospect ahead of him impressed him vaguely as dangerous, probably threatening some disparagement of the paramount prestige of science.

The writings of Mr. Morris which bear on our discussion are, first, the presentation of his now-famous semantic system, *Foundations of the Theory of Signs,* in Vol. I, No. 2, of the *Encyclopedia*; and, applying his new semantics to art, the two essays, "Science, Art and Technology," in *The Kenyon Review* of Autumn, 1939, and "Aesthetics and the Theory of Signs," in *The Journal of Unified Science,* Vol. VIII.

Mr. Morris as a semanticist finds that all discourse consists in signs, and that any sign functions in three dimensions. There is the *syntactical* dimension, involving all of what we should call its logic; there is the *semantical* dimension proper, involving the reference of the sign to an object; and finally the *pragmatical* dimension, involving whatever reference there may be in the sign, implicit or explicit, to its psychological, biological, and sociological uses. I cannot here enlarge upon this outline. There is no short cut to Mr. Morris's knowledge; his own account will need to be read, and then reread. I think it will appear to the reader that he has a genius for fixing sound distinctions, and imposes order on a field that has hitherto been filled with confusion. I have but one source of hesitation. I do not quite sense the coördinate equality, as a component in the sign-functioning, of the pragmatical dimension with the other two. It is like according a moral dimension to poetry because there are some poems which not only present their own content but in addition moralize about this content. We may reflect that they need not do so, and that many other poems do not, and that the moral value we may find for the poem seems somewhat external to the poem itself. But at any rate Mr. Morris makes the pragmatical dimension quite distinct from the others, if not subsidiary, and that is something. Science, in Mr. Morris's view, need not be very conscious of any pragmatics; and so it may be, in our view, with art; really it is technology, or applied science, that is decidedly pragmatical.

For Mr. Morris not only distinguishes three irreducible dimensions of meaning, but finds as well three irreducible forms of discourse: science, art, and technology. These seem to him to emphasize respectively the semantical, the syntactical, and the pragmatical dimensions. To us, as I have just remarked, art may seem specially affiliated with science, and further away from technology, in not having any necessary concern with pragmatics or usefulness. But in another sense it is closer to tech-

4

nology and further from science. We recall our old impression, or perhaps we recall our knowledge of the Greek philosophers, to the effect that art, like technology, is concerned with making something, as well as knowing something; while pure science seems concerned only with knowing something. And what poetry makes—and the word means a making—is the poem, which at least in respect to its meter is a peculiarly novel and manufactured form, and obviously a rather special unit of discourse.

With regard to the credibility of aesthetic discourse, Mr. Morris pronounces handsomely enough: like scientific discourse, it is objective, and knowledge-giving. He says:

> It is true, I believe, that the aesthetic sign, in common with all signs, has all three dimensions of sign-functioning; such a position seems a wise corrective to the common but too simple view that the artist simply "emotes" or "expresses himself" without any concern for actuality.

But if art as knowledge seems to Mr. Morris capable of the same sort of validity that science has, and at times to be indistinguishable from science in this respect, it has a remarkable differentia, and is forever unlike science, in the following respect. The sign which science employs is a mere sign, or "symbol," that is, an object having no other character—for the purpose of discourse at least—than that of referring to another object which is its semantical object. For example, symbols are algebraic characters; or words used technically, as defined in the dictionary, or defined for the purpose of a given discourse in the discourse itself. But the aesthetic signs are "icons," or images. As signs they have semantical objects, or refer to objects, but as iconic signs they also resemble or imitate these objects.

The significance of this distinction that immediately flashes upon us, though it does not seem to be noticed by Mr. Morris,

5

is that the object symbolized by a scientific sign would seem to be abstract, as, for example, a single property or aspect of objects, whereas the object symbolized by an iconic or aesthetic sign must be a whole object. And even if both seem to refer to the whole object, and the same object, there is a difference; if, for example, the scientific sign is of "man," the iconic sign is of "this particular man." By general convention the man of scientific discourse is the definable and "essential" man, whose definition involves a single set of values which are constant and negotiable for logical discourse. The man of the iconic sign is evidently imitable, or imaginable, but not definable. In brief, under the iconic sign the abstract item is restored to the body from which it was taken.

The iconic character of aesthetic signs is given by Mr. Morris in a rather matter-of-fact sort of testimony; yet it is almost the more impressive just because he does not draw the exciting implications. It amounts to a late restoration of the old doctrine of art as "imitation," to which Plato and Aristotle adhered, but which most modern aestheticians have abandoned as something absurdly simple. "Imitation" is a commonplace locution, but may be thought unworthy of the aesthetic occasion; yet I can imagine our aestheticians solemnly accepting the doctrine of "icons" because it sounds technical; actually of course it is one of the two ordinary terms in which the Greeks rendered the idea of imitation. And since Mr. Morris is affiliated in the project of the *Encyclopedia* with naturalist, positivist, and pragmatist philosophers, I think of this enlightened testimony as another evidence of what I have hoped for: the capacity of radical modernist philosophy to apprehend and testify to kinds of truth that do not necessarily suit its own preoccupations, which are scientific ones.

It is sometimes difficult to say what is being "represented" by an aesthetic icon; in music, for example, or in a poem which makes discourse without very often referring specifically to concrete material objects. We think of "reflective" poetry which is truly poetry, and is imaginative, and yet probably a little deficient in brilliant object-images. Mr. Morris makes no question but that any variety of poetry employs iconic signs. (He offers at one point an analysis of "abstract" painting for the purpose of showing that it denotes ultimately the structure of the natural world.)

It is less difficult, and I believe Mr. Morris does not remark this problem, to see how the poem, which is a discourse in words, may offer icons as easily as painting does. The icons here are in the mind, they are the mental images evoked. The technical use of language by the poet is one that lifts words out of their symbolic or definitive uses into imaginative or image-provoking uses.

3

And that is almost as far as Mr. Morris goes. He claims that art is especially interested in the syntactical dimension of discourse, but offers almost no study of how art makes a syntax out of its peculiar mixture of pure symbols and liberal iconic signs. That would become a study of almost monumental significance. Is its validity comparable with that of science? Is its syntactical validity comparable with its own semantical validity, which Mr. Morris is good enough to accept as beyond question?

Science deals exclusively in pure symbols, but art deals essentially, though not exclusively, in iconic signs. This makes at once a sharp formal or technical distinction between the two forms of discourse; but one would think it must become also a philosophical distinction. Mr. Morris elicits chiefly the consequence that no treatment of the arts can be included within the *Encyclopedia of Unified Science.* Only semeiotic, the theory of signs, which makes its own entry as prefatory to the body of the work, may remark for the sake of formal exclusion upon the contrasted arts. But one might think that semeiotic required a closer and therefore surer study of the arts than that; for example, a study of the question why science did not choose, or had not the constitutional capacity, to employ iconic signs also; and, of course, of the ontological question itself, respecting the grades of content that the two discourses handled through their different sorts of signs, and the elemental or categorical nature of scientific knowledge as determined through the comparison with aesthetic knowledge.

In the independent essays outside the *Encyclopedia* Mr. Morris does offer some results of his own study. They seem to me inadequate. For example:

> The view proposed is that the aesthetic sign designates the value properties of actual or possible situations and that it is an iconic sign (an "image") in that it embodies these values in some medium where they may be directly inspected (in short, the aesthetic sign is an iconic sign whose designatum is a value). To give content to this statement it would be necessary to analyze in detail the notion of value and the characteristics of iconic signs, but this is neither practical nor advisable in the present context. For whatever theory of value be maintained, it must be recognized that objects have value properties among their total set of properties (an object can be insipid, sublime, menacing, oppressive, or gay in some contexts just as it may have a certain mass or length or velocity in other contexts) and that aesthetic media, since they themselves are objects, can embody certain value properties

(a small piece of cork could hardly be sublime, but it could be insipid or even gay).

Here it seems to me that Mr. Morris in effect is about to recant from his doctrine of the icons. The icon here is only a medium denoting, by embodying, a value; but that is more than a symbol does; he should say that the icon is a body imitating some actual embodiment of the value. And what value? I do not think he makes it clear, even with the help of his illustrations, how an icon embodies a value-property, or what sorts of values aesthetic discourse ordinarily is interested in. Certainly it sounds as if the aesthetic value-properties were quite different from the scientific ones; gaiety and sublimity, among others, for aesthetic value-properties, mass and velocity for scientific ones. It is rather suspicious that several of the aesthetic value-properties mentioned might be said to be affective ones, whereas the scientific value-properties mentioned are objective physical ones; so that Mr. Morris's aesthetic theory looks at this point like another version of affective or psychologistic theory. But we require much more detail from him about all this.

Briefly, may we say that the observations of Mr. Morris are promising, and even exciting: aesthetic discourse is objective knowledge, and its constituent signs have the remarkable character of being icons. But the sequel is disappointing. An icon merely embodies some certain value-property or other; that is all we are told about its operation. And as to the human significance, the usefulness or pragmatical function, Mr. Morris's imagination is again very timid. For example:

> . . . the scientists may be helped in the scientific study of values by the vivid portrayal of the value whose conditions he endeavors to trace.

And similarly:

The technologist in turn can only be grateful for the vivid presentation of the values whose status in nature he attempts to control.

The artist is pictured here as furnishing the icons which embody the precise and single scientific values, not the values causing the massive affective states referred to in the previous quotation. But his virtue seems to lie solely in the technical assistance, or else the moral encouragement, which his icons lend to the scientist and technologist in their need.

The aesthetic project has turned out rather small and ignominious after its fine beginnings in Mr. Morris's hands.

We might sketch here, though tentatively and rudely, a really ontological argument, such as Mr. Morris's preliminaries seemed to invite.

The validity of a scientific discourse depends in part, we should say, on its semantical purity. That is, each symbol should refer to an object specifically defined, or having a specific value-aspect, for the discourse; and throughout the discourse it should have exactly that reference and no other. The reference of a single symbol is limited, and uniform.

In aesthetic discourse, however, we replace symbols with icons; and the peculiarity of an icon is that it refers to the whole or concrete object and cannot be limited. As Mr. Morris says, an icon "embodies" the value-property that is the object of discourse. But "embodies" is a great word, and Mr. Morris ought to accept its consequences. Certainly he offers no rule as to how the value-property may be isolated in the body of the containing icon, or placed in the center, or otherwise made to stand out so that we shall be sure to attend to it rather than to the containing body.[1]

[1] It is true that in one context he talks about the icon as representing a "consummatory" or final value, as if constituting the image of a body

The icon is an individual, therefore indefinable; that is, it exceeds definition. In the play, the icon is our image of Prince Hamlet, and it is never twice the same, so that the rule of consistent definitive reference is abrogated with each reappearance. An individual has too many properties, and too many values. If a kind of discourse is accredited (and given a semantical bill of health) which proposes to deal in particulars, as one must propose to do which deals in icons, then it is removed far indeed from scientific discourse; it decidedly invites philosophical attention, and one must be prepared to make dispositions which are heroic, because in the present state of theory they will be novel.

The syntactical dimension is imperiled, upon the introduction of icons into discourse, along with the semantical. It will be impossible for discourse to compel its icons to function in the strict logic which we have learned to expect from the symbols. The logic of art will probably be variable in the degree of its validity, but always in degree lower than that of science. At the same time we shall probably incline to assert that it will have no validity at all unless it holds itself together at least in part by scientific symbols. So the aesthetic discourse will be discovered, one expects, making digressions from its logic with its icons at local points; or perhaps maintaining itself on the whole in terms of valid symbols, but occasionally and suddenly building a routine symbol out into the icon denoting the full

---

so obviously meant for consumption, so ripe for immediate consumption, that nobody could resist knowing the value it meant to put forward. But even so I do not know what the body is for. The body is an impediment, and has to be waived, in order to attend to the value that interests the consumer, or even the strict discourser. But it is much easier to suppose that the body is there to be attended to as much as the value; and that attention to the body may not be characteristic of scientific discourse, but is the distinguishing characteristic of aesthetic discourse.

body of the object of which the symbol denotes only a single value-property. But the semantics and the syntactics of art together invite the most exacting study if we care to identify them really.

In scientific discourse we deal with a single value-system at a time. In art only the paraphrase, of which Mr. Morris gives an edequate account, and which is the "moral," the theme, or the argument of the discourse, offers the single-value system; the work itself goes beyond its paraphrase into the realm of the natural objects or situations themselves, which are many-valued.

Art as a discourse, indeed, is anomalous, and all but incredible; a discourse which looks legitimate so long as it looks merely scientific, but every moment or so turns up its icons, in which it hardly seems that discourse could take place.

Science, as Mr. Morris says, is statemental, and its statements have predictive value. But art employs icons, which being individual are contingent and unpredictable. Art seems to permit us to predict only some order of unpredictability.

But principles of this sort are ontological. The world of predictability, for example, is the restricted world of scientific discourse. Its restrictive rule is: one value at a time. The world of art is the actual world which does not bear restriction; or at least defies the restrictiveness of science, and offers enough fullness of content to give us the sense of the actual objects. A qualitative density, or value-density, such as is unknown to scientific understanding, marks the world of the actual objects. The discourse which tries systematically to record this world is art.

As to the pragmatics of the poetic act, or its "psychological, biological, and social" motivation, I have almost nothing to suggest. It seems very idle to assume, as Mr. Morris does in effect, that the pragmatical intention of art is the same as that of science; we would ask him why scientists should not commit themselves then to aesthetic as well as scientific discourse. But the psychologists have not furnished us with decisive motivations for this as for many other acts. It is an act of knowledge. The scientific and aesthetic ways of knowledge should illuminate each other; perhaps they are alternative knowledges, and a preference for one knowledge over the other might indicate an elemental or primary bias in temperament. But even if the pragmatical sanction behind the act has to be improvised, and psychologically is less than regular, nevertheless it seems certain that the act is imperative.

4

At this point I venture to abandon the framework of Mr. Morris's speculations. They have provided considerable moral reinforcement for the inquiry. I wish to start a little further back in the ontological analysis of the poem.

The critic of a poem knows that the labor of composing it was, at the least, a verbal exercise in search of a language which on the one hand would "make the sense," and on the other hand would "make the rhythm," and if it liked would even "make the rhyme." He knows it so well that perhaps he is past being curious about the fact.

But it is still strange to us, who are not agreed on any standard version of the natural history of the form, that poetry should ever have coveted a language that would try to do not one hard thing but two hard things at once. Extravagant exercises with language are not the rule by which the logical men have arrived at their perfections of thought. But the composition of a poem is an operation in which an argument fights to displace a meter, and the meter fights to displace the argument.

It would seem that the sacrifices made on both sides would be legible forever in the terms of peace, which are the dispositions found in the finished poem, where the critic must analyze them if he thinks they further the understanding of poetry. Most critics seem to think it does not, for they do not try the analysis, nor the philosophical speculations it might suggest. On the contrary, it is common for critics to assume that a good poet is in control of his argument, and that the meter has had no effect on it, or if anything points its logic all the better, and that the form of the argument is perfect.

If the unsatisfactoriness of poetic theory, which strikes us so painfully, is due to the absence from it of radical philosophical generalities, the fault must begin really with its failure to account for the most elementary and immediate aspect that formal poetry wears: its metrical form. The convention of the metrical form is thought to be as old as the art itself. Perhaps it is the art itself. I suggest that the meter-and-meaning process is the organic act of poetry, and involves all its important characters.

Let us suppose a lady who wishes to display a bowl of fruits upon her sideboard and says to her intelligent houseboy: "Go to the box of apples in the pantry and select and bring me a dozen of the biggest and reddest ones." The box contains a hundred apples, which vary both in bigness and in redness. And we will suppose, as it is easy to suppose, that there is no definable correlation between the bigness and the redness; a big apple is not necessarily a red one, and vice versa. The boy interests himself in the curious problem, and devises the following solution.

He ranges the apples first in order of their bigness, and denotes the biggest as B_1, the next as B_2, and so on down to B_{100}. Then he ranges the apples in order of their redness, and denotes the reddest as R_1, the next reddest as R_2, and so on

14

down to R_{100}. Then for each apple he adds the numerical co-efficient of its bigness and the numerical coefficient of its red-ness; for example, the apple which is tagged B_1 is also tagged R_{36}, so that its combined coefficient is 37. He finds the twelve apples with lowest combined coefficients and takes them to his mistress.

She will have to concede, as he has conceded, that objects systematically valued for two unrelated properties at once are likely not to be superlative in both properties. She will not secure the perfection of her object in one aspect if she is also trying to secure its perfection in another aspect. She has com-mitted herself to a two-ground basis of selection, and her selections on the one ground have to accommodate themselves to her selections on the other ground. It is a situation in which some compromises are necessary.

But she may find an unexpected compensation. In regretting the loss of certain nearly solid-red apples, which are denied to her because they are little, she may observe that the selected ap-ples exhibit color patterns much more various, unpredictable, and interesting. She finds pleasure in studying their markings, whereas she would have obtained the color-value of her solid-red apples at a glance.

I am sorry to think that no such compensation appears for her putting up with second-best apples in the respect of size; which is a stupid category. But I am afraid the analogy of the bigness-redness relation in apples does not represent sufficiently the meter-meaning relation which we are to examine in poetry.

5

Much more difficult than the selection of apples that shall be both big and red is the composition of a poem on the two-ground basis of (1) an intended meaning and (2) an intended meter. In theory the feat seems impossible, unless we are allowed to introduce some qualifications into the terms. It is true that language possesses two properties, the semantic and the phonetic; that is, respectively, the property of referring under fairly fixed conventions to objects beyond itself, which constitute its meaning, and the property of being in itself a sequence of objective physical sounds set to an elementary music.

I assume that there is hardly necessity for an extended argument to the effect that a perfect metrical construction, of which the components were words selected from the range of all actual words, and exclusively for phonetic effects, would not be likely to make noteworthy sense. It would be nonsense. Nor for another argument to show that a pure logical construction would not be likely to make meter. The latter case we have with us always, in our science, in the prose of our newspapers and business correspondence, in our talk. Even so, there might be some instruction in considering for a moment such a little piece of mathematical discourse as this:

$$(a + b)^2 = a^2 + 2ab + b^2$$

Here the mathematician is saying exactly what he means, and his language is not metrical, and we can discover if we try that he does not want any poet to meter it, on the matter-of-fact ground that the poet would have to take liberties with his logical values. At once a question or two should present themselves very vexingly to the nebulous aesthetician: What sort of liberties does the poet take with a discourse when he sets it to meter? And what sort of discourse is prepared to permit those liberties?

An argument which admits of alteration in order that it may

receive a meter must be partly indeterminate. The argument cannot be maintained exactly as determined by its own laws, for it is going to be undetermined by the meter.

Conversely, a metrical form must be partly indeterminate if it proposes to study an argument. It is useless to try to determine it closely in advance, for the argument will un-determine it.

The second principle, of the two just stated, may seem the less ominous. To most poets, and most readers, the meaning is more important than the meter.

Let DM stand for determinate meaning, or such of the intended meaning as succeeds in being adhered to; it may be fairly represented by the logical paraphrase of the poem. IM stands for indeterminate meaning, or that part of the final meaning which took shape not according to its own logical necessity but under metrical compulsion; it may be represented by the poem's residue of meaning which does not go into the logical paraphrase. DS stands for the determinate sound-structure, or the meter; and IS stands for whatever phonetic character the sounds have assumed which is indeterminate.

In theory, the poem is the resultant of two processes interacting upon each other; they come from opposite directions. On the one hand the poet is especially intent upon his meter, DS, which may be blocked out as a succession of unaccented and accented syllables arranged in lines, perhaps with rhyme endings; but there is DM, a prose discourse, which must be reduced into the phonetic pattern; his inclination is to replace its words with others from the general field of words which suit the music, and without much regard for their logical propriety. But he is checked on the other hand where he starts with firm possession of DM, a prose meaning, but has to assimilate it to DS, the sound-pattern that he has chosen; his inclination is to replace the required metrical sounds with others that suit his logic and are not quite so good for the sound-structure.

Actually, a skillful piece of composition will have many stages of development, with strokes too subtle and rapid to record, and operations in some sort of alternation from the one direction and the other. The poet makes adaptations both of sound to meaning (introducing IS) and of meaning to sound (introducing IM). Both adaptations are required for the final version of the poem.

6

The most interesting observation for the critic, perhaps, is that the poem is an object comprising not two elements but four; not merely a meaning M, but DM, that part of a meaning which forms a logical structure, and IM, a part which does not belong to the structure and may be definitely illogical, though more probably it is only additive and a-logical; and not merely DS, a sound-pattern, but IS, a part of the total sound-effect which may be in exception to the rule but at any rate does not belong to it. These elements are familiar enough to the poet himself, who has manipulated them. Frequently they are evident to the critic too. They should be, very substantially; they can be distinguished to the extent that he is capable of distinguishing them. Logically they are distinct elements, now, in the finished poem, though it may not be possible to trace back the precise history of their development under the tension of composition.

I cannot but think that the distinction of these elements, and especially of DM and IM, is the vocation par excellence of criticism. It is more technical than some other exercises which go as criticism, but more informed. It brings the criticism of poetry to somewhat the same level of professional competence as that of the discussions which painters sometimes accord to paintings, and that which musicians accord to music; which means, I think, an elevation of our normal critical standard.

If a poet is a philosopher, explicitly or implicitly, treating matters of ethical or at least human importance—and it is likely that he is that—the discussion of his "ideology" may be critical in every sense in which one may be said to criticize systematic ideas; but the ideas of the poet, struggling but not quite managing to receive their really determinate expression, are only his DM, and a better version is almost certain to be found elsewhere in prose, so that their discussion under the poem is likely to be a tame affair. Few poets serve, as Wordsworth and Shelley may be thought to do, as texts for the really authoritative study of ideas; mostly they serve amateur ideologists for that purpose, or serve distinguished critics who fall back upon this sort of thing because nothing is quite prescriptive in their vocation. The more interesting thing to study is the coexistence and connection of DM and IM—the ideas and the indeterminate material in which they are enveloped. This kind of study is much severer, but its interest is profounder and more elemental than the merely ethical; it is an ontological interest.

Possibly an examination of poetry along these lines might finally disclose the secret of its strange yet stubborn existence as a kind of discourse unlike any other. It does not bother too much about the perfection of its logic; and does bother a great deal, as if it were life and death, about the positive quality of that indeterminate thing which creeps in by the back door of musical necessity. I suggest the closest possible study of IM, the indeterminate meaning.

But there are two kinds of indeterminacy in IM, and I wish to show how the poet in metering his argument yields reluctantly to the first, as to an indeterminacy that means only inaccuracy and confusion, and then gladly to the second, as to an indeterminacy that opens to him a new world of discourse.

First, he tries to shift the language within the range of a rough verbal equivalence, and to alter DM no more substantively than necessary. A given word will probably have synonyms. The order of words in a phrase may be varied. A transitive predication may be changed to a passive; a relative clause to a participial phrase. In the little words denoting logical connections and transitions a good deal of liberty may be taken without being fatal; they may be expanded into something almost excessively explicit, or they may be even omitted, with the idea that the reader can supply the correct relations. A single noun may become a series of nouns, or nearly any other element may be compounded, without introducing much novelty. Epithetical adjectives and adverbs may be interpolated, if they will qualify their nouns and verbs very obviously. Archaic locutions may be substituted for contemporary ones. A poet is necessarily an accomplished verbalist, and capable of an almost endless succession of periphrases that come nearer and nearer to metered language until finally he achieves what he wants; a language that is metrical enough, and close to his intended meaning.

Mr. C. D. Abbott at the library of the University of Buffalo is collecting a very large number of work sheets from living poets, with the idea of securing an objective exhibit of the actual process of perfecting poems by revision. The most immediate use of these manuscripts that will suggest itself will surely be the critical study of the way poets tinker with given phrases in order to adapt them to the metrical pattern. Presently there should be a voluminous bulk of evidence on this point. But anybody who has tried versification can predict the sort of evidence that will turn up. Meanwhile we may see what evidences there are in the final poems themselves.

Wordsworth would probably be cited by the historian as one who metered his language with more method than inspiration, especially in his longer work. Here is a passage from the *Prelude,* where he is talking about the power of poetry, and its habitation in a place called "the mystery of words":

> . . . there,
> As in a mansion like their proper home,
> Even forms and substances are circumfused
> By that transparent veil with light divine,
> And through the turnings intricate of verse
> Present themselves as objects recognized
> In flashes, and with glory not their own.

It is easy to find disagreeable lapses of logic here. There are the painful inversions of order, clearly in the interest of metric: *light divine* and *turnings intricate.* The line *As in a mansion like their proper home* is certainly a curious involution for *As in a mansion which is their proper home.* The third and fourth lines are not transparent for us like the veil talked about: Does the veil possess and give off the divine light? And if not, how does it circumfuse the forms and substances with it? The brevity of statement is either a laziness on Wordsworth's part, or it is a recourse to elliptical expression invited by metrical exigencies. But at this point all our little objections pass into a big and overwhelming one: there is really in this passage scarcely any specific discourse of respectable logical grade. We do not know what any of these pretty things is, or does. No prose would be cynical enough to offer so elusive a content. The mansion, the forms and substances, the magic veil, the divine light, the movement of the turnings, the flashes and the borrowed glory—these look like responsible and promising objects, but none of them establishes a sufficient identity when they all assemble together. The poet became a little paralyzed, we may imagine, when he took pen in hand to write a poem; or got that way after going a certain distance in the writing of a long one. I go beyond the direct evidence here, but I assume that making distinguished metrical discourse was such a job, and consisted in his own mind with so much corruption of the sense at best, that he fell into the habit of choosing the most resounding words, and stringing them together as the meter dictated. This is not unusual in Romantic poetry. The point to make about Romantic poetry now is not the one about its noble words, but a negative and nasty one: the noble words are almost absurdly incoherent. (But I realize that my tone is too severe.)

Pope was not a Romantic, and I suppose the language has known no poet more nice in his expression. I quote:

> Close by those meads, forever crowned with flowers,
> Where Thames with pride surveys his rising towers,
> There stands a structure of majestic frame,
> Which from the neighboring Hampton takes its name.
> Here Britain's statesmen oft the fall foredoom
> Of foreign tyrants and of nymphs at home;
> Here thou, great Anna! whom three realms obey,
> Dost sometimes counsel take—and sometimes tea.

With so great a master of language, it is a little dangerous to insist on the exact place where the meter coming in drove some of the logic out. But the superiority of his logic over Wordsworth's is not so overwhelming as it seems; for the most part it is merely that his improvisations are made to look nearly natural, as if he thoroughly intended them all the time, and meter

22

had nothing to do with them. The *flowers* is arrived at gracefully, but the chief source of any "inevitability" claimed for it is the fact that it rhymes with *towers,* which is more important to the discourse. In four lines we come to Hampton Court, where will presently appear Belinda, whom we have left traveling in her boat on the Thames. Hampton Court has a location with respect to the Thames which we need to know, under the principles of the logical or narrative argument; and at Hampton Court assemble the royalty and the fashionable gentry, whom we must know too; these are among the necessary moves. Hampton Court is close by those *rising towers* which are London-on-Thames, and that is enough as to its location; it is a matter of course that it will be close by the meads, since the towers will rise out of the meads by the river rather than rise out of the river. If we should invert the two lines, as follows,

> Near where proud Thames surveys his rising towers,
> And where are meads forever crowned with flowers,

something would happen not only to the euphony of the language but to the respectability of its logic, for then it would be plain that the meads-and-flowers line is chiefly useful for filling up a couplet. But the next couplet lacks honest logical economy too. The *structure of majestic frame* is nothing but a majestic structure, with a rhyme tag added, and the account of the naming of Hampton Court is a metrical but logically gratuitous expansion of the simple recital of its name. The other two couplets both employ rhyme words, and contexts to assimilate them, which are so incongruous that they have to be employed in discourse as the occasions of wit. As logicians we need not take much stock in wit as forwarding argument, even when it is free from suspicion as a device to look after difficult rhyme pairings; it supposes such a lack of an obvious logical relation between two things that any technical bridge of connection must be accepted. No honest "argument" prefaced to a poem would cover the poet's witticisms. We condemn Romantic poets for injecting their burning sentiments into an objective argument, but other poets are given to wit, which is likewise at the expense of argument and logic.[2] A final remark will sound a little captious. Hampton Court is in mind, but the word "Court" is not used and possibly its absence troubles the poet; at any rate if he does not have a court he supplies the short passage with three royalties. There is the lady of the meads, a figurative queen, with a crown of flowers; Thames, a figurative patriarch, and at least a prince with all his rising towers (though a little while earlier there was a feminine character of the same name upon whose "silver bosom" Belinda rode in her boat); and actual Queen Anne. It seems an excessive profusion of royalties.

There are certainly readers of the Binomial Theorem who are prohibited by conscience from the reading of poetry; we have just been looking at some of the reasons. On these terms meter may be costing more than it is worth. Milton thought of the possibility, and went so far as to renounce its most binding device, the rhyme; it is employed by

[2] Mr. Cleanth Brooks reproves the sentimentality of simple poets, but puts himself rather off guard by his blanket counterendorsement of the wit of university or sophisticated poets. If we had an aesthetician's version of Horace's fable of the town mouse and the country mouse, we would be sure to find the latter uttering countrified sentimental discourse, and scorned by the other; but the discourse of the town mouse not only would be smart, it would presently become oversmart, and silly; so that in the long run we should smile at her as at the country cousin, and for much the same reason: naïveté, as plain in personal vanity as in simplicity. Elizabethan comedy finds its butt in the smart town character as readily as in the country simpleton.

Some famous modern Poets, carried away by Custom, but much to their own vexation, hindrance, and constraint to express many things otherwise, and for the most part worse, than else they would have expressed them.

But greater purists might apply this logic to all the rest of the metrical devices. We turn to Milton's own unrhymed verse, and find:

> Thus, while he spake, each passion dimm'd his face
> Thrice chang'd with pale, ire, envy and despair,
> Which marr'd his borrow'd visage, and betray'd
> Him counterfeit, if any eye beheld.

The argument of this narrative passage would explain how Uriel, deceived once by Satan in his "stripling cherub's" disguise, perceives now his identity through the satanic passions registered in his face, and initiates the next cycle of action by informing the angels guarding Paradise. But the language, as is not uncommon with Milton, from the point of view of logic is almost like a telegraphic code in its condensation, and omission of connectives; it is expansible to two or three times its length in prose, and readable only with difficulty by unaccustomed readers. Yet it also lapses from strict logic in precisely the opposite direction, by the importation of superfluous detail. The three successive increments of pallor and their respective causes would seem beyond the observation of Uriel, in the sun, and in fact we learn presently that what Uriel actually marked was Satan's "gestures fierce" and "mad demeanor." Milton is aware of this, and gives himself a technical alibi in our passage by being careful to say that the pallor stages betrayed the fraud not necessarily to Uriel but to any good eye that might be close enough to see them. Still, if Uriel did not see them they do not matter.

It would have been hard to persuade Milton out of this passage, with its deficiencies and superfluities; but suppose we might have proposed an alternative version, which would seem safely eclectic and within the traditional proficiencies of poetry; and I shall not mind appearing ridiculous for the sake of the argument:

> Speaking, rank passion swelled within his breast
> Till all the organism felt its power,
> And such a pallor in his face was wrought
> That it belied the angelic visage fair
> He had assumed. Uriel, unsleeping guard,
> With supernatural vision saw it plain.

But Milton in his turn would instantly have gibed at it, and on our terms; at the dangling participle and the poetic inversion, as violations of good syntax; and then at the constant tendency, perhaps proceeding from our nervous desire to come with some spirit out of an embarrassing situation, to exceed the proper logical content, as shown in all four first lines by the verbs, *swelled, felt, was wrought,* and *belied.* They are ambitious, and start our minds upon little actions that would take us out of the plane of the argument.

Returning to rhymed verse, there is this passage from a poem which deserves its great fame, but whose fabulous "perfections" consist with indeterminacies that would be condemned in the prose of scientists, and also of college freshmen; though I think in the prose of college seniors they might have a different consideration:

> Had we but world enough, and time,
> This coyness, lady, were no crime.
> We would sit down, and think which way
> To walk, and pass our long love's day.

Thou by the Indian Ganges' side
Should'st rubies find: I by the tide
Of Humber would complain. I would
Love you ten years before the flood,
And you should, if you please, refuse
Till the conversion of the Jews;
My vegetable love should grow
Vaster than empires and more slow.

I will use the pedagogical red pencil, though I am loath. World, as distinguished from time, is not space, for the lovers already have all the space in the world, and long tenure would not increase it. It is a violent condensation meaning, I think, "the whole history of the world before us," and combining with the supposal of their having time to live through it; it supports the historical references which follow. *We would, thou should'st, my love should:* the use of the auxiliaries is precise, varying according to rule from person to person, and uniformly denoting determination or command: "we would arrange it so." But it is remarkable that in so firm a set of locutions, which attests the poet's logical delicacy, the *thou should'st* is interchangeable with *you should;* the meter is responsible for the latter version, since otherwise we should have the line, *And thou should'st, if thou pleased'st, refuse;* or, taking the same liberty with tenses which we find actually taken (again for metrical reasons), *And thou should'st, if thou pleas'st, refuse;* but either line clogs the meter. *Which way* is one phrase, but language is an ambiguous thing, and it has two meanings: *in which direction* as applied to *walk,* and *in what manner* as applied to *pass our day.* The parallel series in lines 5–7 is in three respects not uniform: *Ganges* has little need of a defining adjective, except the metrical one, but when once it has become *Indian Ganges* there is every right on the part of its analogue to be styled *English Humber;* and

Ganges' side calls for *Humber's side,* or for merely *Humber's,* with *side* understood, but rhyme produces for Humber a *tide;* and the possessive case in the first member would call for the same in the second member, but is replaced there actually by an *of*-phrase. *Refuse* brings out of the rhyming dictionary the *Jews,* which it will tax the poet's invention to supply with a context; but for our present purposes the poet has too much invention, for it gives him the historical period from the Flood to the conversion of the Jews, which is a handsome way of saying ten thousand years, or some other length of time, and seems disproportionate to the mere ten years of the same context, the only other period mentioned. *Vegetable* is a grotesque qualification of love, and on the whole decidedly more unsuitable than suitable, though there are features in which it is suitable. *Vaster* would correlate with *slower,* but not with *more slow;* but they would not be correlatives at all after *grow,* for *vaster* is its factitive complement and *slower* can only be for *more slowly,* its adverb. Finally, there is the question of how the vastness of the poet's love can resemble the vastness of empires; the elegance of the terms seems to go along with the logic of a child.

7

But the important stage of indeterminacy comes, in the experiment of composition, when the imagination of the poet, and not only his verbal mechanics, is engaged. An "irrelevance" may feel forced at first, and its overplus of meaning unwanted, because it means the importation of a little foreign or extraneous content into what should be determinate, and limited; but soon the poet comes upon a kind of irrelevance that seems desirable, and he begins to indulge it voluntarily, as a new and positive asset to the meaning. And this is the principle: the importations which the imagination introduces into discourse have the value of developing the freedom which lurks in the "body," and under the surface, of apparently determinate situations. When Marvell is persuaded by the rhyme consideration to invest the Humber with a tide, or to furnish his abstract calendar with specifications about the Flood, and the conversion of the Jews, he does not make these additions reluctantly. On the contrary, he knows that the brilliance of the poetry depends on the shock, accompanied at once by the realism or the naturalness, of its powerful individuality. But the mere syllabic measure, and not only the rhyme, can induce this effect. When the poet investigates the suitability of a rhyme word for his discourse, he tries the imaginative contexts in which it could figure; but the process is the same when he tries many new phrases in the interest of the rhythm, for their suitability, though his imagination has to do without the sharp stimuli of the rhyme words. And by suitability I mean the propriety which consists in their denoting the proper effect which really belongs to the object. In this way what is irrelevant for one kind of discourse becomes the content for another kind, and presently the new kind stands up firmly if we have the courage to stand by it.

The passages cited above were in support of the negative and corrupt IM, but they illustrate also the positive IM, which is poetic texture, for the critic, and ontological freedom for the philosopher. Wordsworth has the most abstract argument, but instead of pursuing it closely and producing a distinguished logical structure— it might have come to a really superior version of the argument we are here trying to build up, something about the meaning of poetry—he wavers toward some interesting concrete objects, producing a mansion, a veil, a light, and a set of intricate turnings; but here too he is stopped, as if by some puritan inhibition, from looking steadily at his objects to obtain a clear image; so that his discourse is not distinguished either for its argument or for its texture. Pope unquestionably has the narrative gift, which means that he has access to the actual stream of events covered by the abstract argument; he is perhaps one of many poets prefiguring our modern prose fiction, and knows that he may suspend his argument whenever he pleases, provided he may substitute another equally positive content, namely, a subnarrative account of the independent character and history of its items. Milton looks principally like a man out of a more heroic age than Pope, in the casualness and roughness of his indeterminacy, but he is bolder also in the positive detail: nothing in Pope's passage compares with his stopping to name the three specific passions in the mind of Satan, and to imagine each one as turning Satan's visage paler than the one before had left it. As for Marvell, we are unwilling to praise or to condemn the peccadilloes of his logic, and here is a case where we take no account of the indeterminacy of the bad sort that results from the metering process, and distresses so many hardheaded readers. This is all overshadowed, and we are absorbed, by the power of his positive details.

Indeterminacy of this positive or valuable sort is introduced when the images make their entry. It looks as if there might be something very wise in the social, anonymous, and universal provision of metrical technique for poetry. The meter seems only to harm the discourse, till presently it works a radical innovation: it induces the provision of individual icons among the hard-and-fast logical symbols. This launches poetry upon its career.

30

8

The development of metrical content parallels that of meaning. As the resonant meter un-determines the meaning and introduces IM, so in turn the likely meaning un-determines the meter and introduces the variations of IS.

The usual minimum of a meter, in English practice, is a succession of lines having a determinate number of determinate feet, and a foot is some syllabic combination having one accented syllable. The most general consequence is that a unit of phonetic structure—a few lines of blank verse, a stanza of rhymed verse, a sonnet or whole poem sometimes—is superimposed upon a unit of meaning-structure; within it the foot may not coincide with the word or small logical unit, but the two structures use precisely the same constituent language in the long run, and come out at the end together; and this is a summary feat of remarkable coördination, when we approach it with the prejudice of a person used to working in pure structures, that is, in one structure at a time. In reading the poem we have our ear all the time immediately upon the progress of the meter, just as we have our discursive mind all the time on the course of the argument; so that the two structures advance simultaneously if not by the same steps, and every moment or so two steps finish together, and two new steps start together. And what we call a "phrase" is at once a period in the argument and a definable element in the metrical structure, and "phrasing" means to the poet the act of grouping the words to serve the two purposes as simultaneously as possible.

We may suppose that the phonetic effect and the meaning-effect are, in theory, perfectly equal and coördinate. But probably we all have much more interest in the meaning than in the sound. Therefore it is convenient to say that the phonetic effect serves as a sort of texture to the meaning. This is to assign to the meaning an ontological addition.

But within the phonetic effect considered for itself alone we find the poet developing for his meter, which is the regular phonetic structure, its own kind of texture, which consists in the metrical variations. He is driven into this course by considerations exactly the same, except in reverse, as those we have seen compelling him to develop within the meaning a texture of meaning. The latter was forced upon him by the necessity of adapting his meaning to the meter; and this is forced upon him by the necessity of adapting his meter to the meaning. When he cannot further reduce his meaning to language more accurately metrical, he accepts a "last version" and allows the variations to stand. These variations of course present the contingency and unpredictability, or in one word the "actuality," of the world of sound. Many phonetic effects are possible really; and here and there a foot or a phrase holds stubbornly to its alien character and is not quite assimilated to the poet's purpose.

But the texture that is realized within a meter is under conventional restrictions, the like of which have not been formulated for the texture within the meaning. Variations from the meter are permissive, but they must be of certain kinds. I suppose experience has shown, or else there is a strange consent of feeling, that the phrasing of the determinate meaning can always be roughly accomplished if allowed a few permissive variations; that the metrical effects, plus the effects allowed in the variations, make language sufficiently flexible to carry any meaning. Take iambic verse, for example, which is the staple for English. Elizabethan dramatic verse became somewhat loosened up or "Websterized" before it finished; and later Coleridge very nearly got the anapaestic foot adopted as a legitimate variation for the iambic within short rhymed lines. But with such exceptions the poets have confined their metrical departures from iambic verse to the permissive variations with remarkable unanimity. So at least until our own period. There have been many poets recently, including the lettered as well as the unlettered, who have cast off the "bondage" of the meters, and employ them only as they find it convenient, or else make it their rule on principle not to cultivate anything approaching metrical determinateness. But I am talking here about the traditional practice. The critic must take it into account if he cares to discuss the traditional poets; there can be no dispute about that.

Shakespeare wrote,

> Whén to | the sés | sions of | swéet sí | lent thóught
> I sum | mon úp | remém | brance of | thíngs pást,

but we may safely suppose that he was aware of the possibility of many other versions, as for example,

> When síts | my pár | liamént | of sí | lent thóught
> To trý | afrésh | the swéet | remém | bered pást.

The assumption that this version entered his mind is of course improbable for more reasons than one, but at least it represents a common situation: the option between a fairly determinate meaning consisting with a variant or indeterminate meter, and a revised and less determinate meaning leading to a more determinate meter. Decision is in favor of the former alternative, but it is in the light of the fact that the metrical variations are all permissive and conventional. Here they consist in the following substitutions: a trochaic for the first iambic of the first line; a double foot or ionic for the third and fourth iambics of that line; and a double foot or ionic for the fourth and fifth iambics of the second line. But the meaning is slightly more severe than the alternative meaning, and Shakespeare does not care to tinker with it. In the alternative version the boldness of the figure may be too odd; and even in that version the third foot of the first line would have in *párliamént* an extra syllable, unless we take advantage again of the permissions and say it is "accounted for by elision." [3]

In Donne, unless it is in Wyatt, whose meters are very difficult to construe, we have the feeling that we should find indeterminacy of metric carried furthest, sometimes almost to the point of unseating the iambic principle:

> Twó graves | must híde | thine and | my córse;
>
> If óne | might, déath | were nó | divórce.

The difficulty of the first line is that every one of the monosyllables, except possibly *and,* is capable of taking a strong logical accent. We do not in fact know how to read it; we do know that the line from which it is in variation is iambic tetrameter; see the following line, completing the couplet, which is dutifully regular. We assign therefore some reading, almost arbitrary, which perhaps metrifies the line sufficiently and respects its structural logic, and we think of that perverseness in Donne which led him so often to mock the law without technically breaking it. Perverseness, that is, as Ben Jonson construed it; and by any account an insubordinacy, or an individualism, which was reluctant to conform, and seemed to offer the pretense that a meaning was involved which was too urgent to tamper with in the interest of meter. But we can

---

[3] The three permissive variations in iambic verse have now all been named: trochaic for iambic, ionic for two iambics, and extra syllable accounted for by elision.

34

defend the substantive orthodoxy of this poet's metrical technique if we should hear complaint against the following line; it has ten syllables, and is shown by its context to be intended for an iambic pentameter:

Blásted | with síghs, | and súr | róunded | with téars.

The parallelism of *with sighs* and *with tears* suggests that the participles on which they depend are also closely coupled; if we are blasted by the sighs, as by winds, we ought to be fairly drowned by the tears, as by floods. But this last is precisely what *surrounded* means. It is from the French *suronder* (Lat. *superundare*), to overflow. The verb in its weak modern sense could hardly find room for two logical accents, and the iambic structure might collapse; but then the logical structure would be impaired too, because it would come in this word to a foolish anticlimax. The only proper reader of the line is the one who trusts the integrity of Donne's metrical intention and looks to see how it can propose to conform here. To this reader the metric is informative. It is strictly the meaning of the line which has determined the variations in the meter, but we have found a meaning which does not destroy the meter, and it is decisive.

Milton is bold in his metric, but his conscience is exacting, and his irregularities come under the conventions. He writes:

Weep nó | more, wóe | ful Shép | herds, wéep | no móre.

The brilliance of this line consists in its falling eventually, and after we have tried other readings in vain, into the entire regularity which was the last thing we expected of it. We are used to receiving the impression, which he likes to give, and which represents a part of the truth, that his determinate meaning

35

produces an indeterminateness in the local meters of nearly every line, even if we understand that this indeterminateness stops at the limits of the permissive convention. Under that impression we were inclined to scan the line this way:

Weep no | more, woe | ful Shep | herds, weep | no more,

which is a metrical line found many times in Milton; but we were troubled over what happened to the logic of the accentless *woeful*. We said to ourselves, however, that the first *weep no more* had precisely the same logical values as the second one. All the same, the *woeful* is really not up to Milton's level as a workman, and we are not content with it. We finally try the normal meter, and we see that Milton intended us to come to it, and thought we must come to it if we believed in his technical competence. In the phrase *weep no more* it is difficult to say that one word has a heavier logical accent than another; yet we cannot accent them all, as we should like to do, and would do in prose. Or can we? The fact is that, reading the line as we finally do, we not only accent all three words but are obliged to: first *no,* then *weep,* then *more;* for the phrase occurs twice. Again the meter is informative. It could not be so if there were not the most minute give-and-take between the meaning and the meter as principles trying to determine each other, and arriving every moment or so at peace with honor, which means careful adjustments by means of reciprocal concessions.

And now I must make an admission that my readers will surely have anticipated. It is not telling the whole truth to say that Shakespeare and other accomplished poets resort to their variations, which are metrical imperfections, because a determinate meaning has forced them into it. The poet likes the variations regardless of the meanings, finding them essential in the capacity of a sound-texture to go with the sound-structure.

36

It is in no very late stage of a poet's advancement that his taste rejects a sustained phonetic regularity as something restricted and barren, perhaps ontologically defective. Accordingly he is capable of writing smooth meters and then roughening them on purpose. And it must be added, while we are about it, that he is capable of writing a clean logical argument, and then of roughening that too, by introducing logical violence into it, and perhaps willful obscurity. We have therefore this unusual degree of complexity in the total structure: the indeterminate sound or the indeterminate meaning, IS or IM, may have been really come to independently, by a poet who senses the aesthetic value of indeterminateness and is veteran enough to go straight after it. But nothing can be introduced into the meaning without affecting the meter, and vice versa; so that IM, and not only DM as was represented in the beginning, un-determines the meter again and produces IS; and, conversely, IS, and not only DS, may un-determine the meaning again and produce IM. It will sound very complicated, but good poets will attest it if we ask them, and I think they will also offer the objective evidences in their poetry if we are skillful enough to read them.

It is necessary to offer some sort of formal disposition of one very large and vague character in the poetic effect: the euphony of the language. Under that head will come the liquidity of the consonantal sequences, which is much more marked in poetry than in prose; the elimination or reduction of harsh consonantal combinations, such as arise naturally in the juxtaposition of words selected on any pure meaning-principle; and the fixing up of the succession of vowel sounds, by way of ensuring variation, or at least avoiding sequences of flat or light vowels. These are working principles of composition also, and naturally they are of effect in un-determining the meaning. To that extent they are structural principles. Doubtless we think of euphony ordinarily as a principle striving for pure luxury of sound; it pleases the musical ear, and we may be sure it pleases also the articulatory sense, even when we read the poem silently. But that is not our kind of argument. Euphony is a sort of last textural refinement within the phonetic dimension of poetry. I believe that in evaluating it we must give "refinement" precedence over "textural." To refine the texture is to make it less perceptible, to make it smoother, to subtract from its private character, and that is to make it consist better with the structure. I incline therefore to think of euphony as a determinate phonetic principle, like meter, though much less binding and interfering in relation to the meaning. Theoretical complications present themselves when we think of it as coming into conflict with meter as a rival structural principle. But I believe we have seen complications enough in this section.

9

And finally we must take account of a belief that is all but universal among unphilosophical critics, and flourishes at its rankest with the least philosophical. It is this: the phonetic effect in a poem not only is (a) metrical and (b) euphonious, but preferably, and very often actually, is (c) "expressive"; that is, offers a sort of sound which "resembles" or partly "is" or at least "suggests" the object that it describes. It is necessary to say rather flatly that the belief is almost completely fallacious; both theoretically on the whole, and specifically in detail, for most of the cases that are cited to prove it. The single word does not in fact resemble appreciably the thing it denotes. The notion that it does is fully disposed of by Mr. I. A. Richards in Chapter III of his *Philosophy of Rhetoric,* assisted by Mr. Leonard Bloomfield's *Language* and Aristotle's *Poetics,* on which Mr. Richard draws for authoritative support. Furthermore, the phrase, or sustained passage, does not in its "movement" resemble the denoted situation at all closely. I do not know any authoritative analysis to cite against this latter form of the fallacy, and I shall not try to improvise one here. I am content—though not all my readers may be—to say that the resemblance usually alleged turns out to be, for hardheaded judges, extremely slight and farfetched; and, to make up for default of argument about this, to offer a little ontological speculation which might make the popular error intelligible by showing what it is really trying to say. There is some sort of truth in even a misstatement.

A wonderful "fitness," harmony, or propriety, even an enduring stability, seems to obtain in the combination of the semantic property and the phonetic property into a fine poetic phrase. It is something we all feel, and I believe it is the fact we need to account for here. But what is the law of its corporate existence? The law is an ontological one: the two properties shall not be identical, or like, homogeneous; they shall be other, unlike, and heterogeneous. It is the law of the actual world everywhere; all sorts of actual things are composed on this principle. It is only the naïve prejudice of our first way of thought, our Eleatic stage of thought, that makes us conceive that the properties must unite by virtue of their sameness. The passage from that stage into the riper stage of thought has its first and most famous description in the discourse of the Eleatic Stranger in Plato's *Sophist*; it has systematic exploitation in Hegel and many other logicians. Red and red will not cohere with each other to make anything but an aggregate of red, nor even do red and yellow make anything astonishing; but red and big, along with a multitude of other properties, heterogeneous properties, cohere into an apple, which is a One formed out of the Many. I suppose we do not understand in any rational sense a particular object, such as an apple, holding together not by

39

mathematical composition but by its own heterogeneity. But we recognize it perceptually. The World of Appearance (or opinion) seemed to Plato inferior to the World of Pure Being (or reason), but he acknowledged that the former was the world which our perceptions took hold of, and indeed was the world of nature.[4]

The poetic phrase is not very much like an apple, and we must concentrate upon that. In what world of discourse does it have its existence? As a thing of sounds it exists in the words; as a thing of meanings it exists in a world beyond the words. The heterogeneity is rather extreme. We recall the old puzzle, the debate on whether the poem resides in the physical words uttered or in the interpretation that is given them. But it exists in both at once; and for fear we forget about the words, they are metered, so that they may be forced upon our attention. One of the "touchstones" used by Matthew Arnold, and fancied by Mr. Eliot and many others, is Dante's line,

In la sua volontade è nostra pace.

But the English translation is only,

In His will is our peace,

which is not a poetic touchstone at all. The meaning is not combined now with the sounds; the words have become mere symbols, used but not incorporated into the object. The line in its English version has suffered ontological annihilation; it has lost one of its worlds. But it seems rather irresponsible to claim that Dante's own version has its superior virtue in the fact that its sound seems to "express" or "suggest" its meaning; though

[4] For the sake of accuracy I should say that the preference was that of Socrates, or of the Plato of the early dialogues.

40

I think I know critics who might be prepared after a little time to argue it, with much circumstance.

The triumphant citations from poetry, the "proofs" that we offer of its power, the touchstones, are always phrases, not single words nor little groups of words; they may be lines, or passages of some lines each. I find more significance in this fact than, merely, that a distinguished piece of logical discourse has to have extension in order to have complexity. It is even true that a compelling phonetic character cannot be imposed upon the words unless there are enough of them to organize into a recognizable meter. Furthermore, and beyond that, the meaning employs the words, but the meter employs the syllables. There is no point-to-point coördination between the development of the semantic structure and that of the phonetic structure. The relation between the two in a poetic phrase seems something like the relation between two melodies in counterpoint, except that our two structures originally look much more heterogeneous than the melodies. Perhaps the aesthetic import of the semantic-phonetic combination is also like that of counterpoint. But I am not sure what profit there is in saying this. It is not obvious that musical aesthetic is much more articulate than literary aesthetic, even allowing for the genius of Schopenhauer. I should think it true of the counterpoint, but at any rate I should judge of the double structure of the poetic phrase, that its force is in its speculative or ontological intimations. The semantic structure alone, like the melody in the treble, may be an aesthetic structure, for it is a logical structure which at the same time admits body, or texture, as pure logical structures do not; yet the phonetic structure, which would seem perfectly unrelated to it, is made to combine with it. It seems a tighter job, stronger, and more wonderful, than the counterpoint can be, for the melodies are two, though they are simultaneous, while the poetic phrase is a single event. Ontologically, it is a case of bringing into experience both a denser and a more contingent world, and commanding a discourse in more dimensions.

10

This has probably gone far enough as an ontological brief in the study of poetic discourse in English. I am aware of its insufficiencies. It is the ontological sense of the traditionalist poets, and their readers, that I have wished to discover. It feels congenial for me.

But what should the ontological critic say about the moderns? Much of our own poetry is conspicuously other than traditional. Not, I believe, the poetry of Robinson, Frost, Bridges, Yeats, perhaps even Hopkins; who have adhered, or almost adhered, or intended to adhere, to the tradition. The poetry I am talking about is written by such poets as Pound, Eliot, Tate, Stevens, perhaps Auden, though I do not mean to list them formally, nor suggest that any of them is uniformly accountable to a critique. These poets are generally known to have high regard for traditionalism, but they make wide and deliberate departures from it for the sake of their own poetry.

The superficial marks of our modernist poetry are very well known. An excellent brief assemblage of them into a list is in "A Note on Poetry," by Mr. Randall Jarrell, prefacing his own verses in *Five Young American Poets*. He considers modernist poetry to be substantially "romantic," and lists its marks, as follows:

> I have no space for the enormous amount of evidence all these generalizations require; but consider some of the qualities of typical modernistic poetry: very interesting language, a great emphasis on connotation, "texture"; extreme intensity, forced

emotion—violence; a good deal of obscurity; emphasis on sensation, perceptual nuances; emphasis on details, on the part rather than the whole; experimental or novel qualities of some sort; a tendency toward external formlessness and internal disorganization—these are justified, generally, as the disorganization required to express a disorganized age, or alternatively, as newly-discovered and more complex types of organization; an extremely personal style—*refine your singularities;* lack of restraint—all tendencies are forced to their limits; there is a good deal of emphasis on the unconscious, dream-structure, the thoroughly subjective; the poet's attitudes are usually anti-scientific, anti-commonsense, anti-public—he is, essentially, removed; poetry is primarily lyric, intensive—the few long poems are aggregations of lyric details; poems usually have, not a logical, but the more or less associational structure of dramatic monologue; and so on and so on.

My notes on this poetry are provisional and unsure, but I shall risk them in order to come down to date. The following account will be the merest sketch of a criticism, and will not even cite any of this poetry specifically.

The fundamental consideration is that the moderns are well instructed in the practice of the traditionalists. But this is what has happened: they find the old practice trite, and ontologically inadequate for them. Yet they lack any consistent conception of what a new practice might be—and a new practice that would be radical enough is probably not possible—and therefore they work by taking liberties with the old practice, and irregularize and de-systematize it, without denying it.

They do not find sufficient profit in that traditional poetic labor which consists in the determinate metering of a determinate discourse. I have argued that some ontological triumph, something impossible for pure discourse, may be secured in this way. They are acquainted with the technique, and find it too easy. The well-metered discourse is impaired for them because it is transparently artful; they want a more direct and less formal knowledge.

They will not tolerate the experience of having the meaning brought by the meter into an indeterminateness of the compelled variety, with the only half-concealed irregularities such as those of Pope and Marvell above, or the resonances like those of the Romantic Wordsworth. Their disaffection is rather advanced. I suppose it is due fundamentally, though paradoxically, to their revulsion against scientific discourse. In seeking a discourse of greater ontological competence they do not propose to exhibit faults that are beneath the enemy standard of performance; and with the rapid and visible perfection of scientific discourse, occurring for the most part since the poetic achievements of the great traditionalists, indeterminateness of the ragged sort can be detected by the literate public everywhere, and is too disreputable. The age of prose, they might argue, has made obsolete the faltering logic of old-fashioned metered poetry. The disabilities of the procedure are too obvious; the advantages promised in it they propose to secure otherwise.

Being technically experienced, they have command of their own imagination, and when they seek indeterminateness of the positive sort, such as is denoted by the iconic signs, they do it directly. They have the power. They manage without the suggestion that comes in the verbal manipulations of metering. Perhaps their imagination, which might otherwise be confined by scientific discourse, has been in the long run released by precisely the kind of poetic exercise described above as elementary in the traditional technique, with meter working functionally in the composition. If so, the moderns might be called the products of a poetic tradition; but they are only its end products; or their status is even posttraditional: they are only the heirs of a tradition.

44

They have no enthusiasm for the meters, with the result that their poetry is far gone in its natural indeterminateness on that side. But they are committed on principle to an unprecedented degree of indeterminateness in the meaning, and their poetry is let down on that side too. This latter indeterminateness yields brilliant images; but it tends to logical inconsequence. The inconsequence does not come from haggling with the meter but from the intractable energy of the images. Evidence of this is that the mode of the inconsequence is chiefly ellipsis: the crowding of the images together without the terms for their logical relations; but also, as we think in view of the honesty of the work, the crowding together very largely without the logical relations themselves. The effect is an ontological density which proves itself by logical obscurity.

The dense and brilliant yet obscure world of the modern poets may reflect a certain initial ontological sense. Their most actual world, as they sense it, resists mastery, is more mysterious than intelligible, perhaps is more evil than good. It is a world of appearances, and suggests, for example, the world of Heraclitus; as if they had knocked the bottom out of history and language and become early Greeks again. They are antipathetic to the modern everyday world of business, science, and positivism, which ontologically disconcerts them. Their early Greek is pluralist, relativist, and irrational.

Their poetry is the manifest of such a skepticism, and virtual if tacit abjuration, as to seem to subject this generation to the category of decadence—if we know enough about the cycle of a culture to apply the term responsibly.

But, for that sense, it probably does not give quite the necessary impression of spent energies. And in that sense it is not quite thorough. A thing that is in startling exception occurs now and then in the practice of every one of the poets: the perfect poetic phrase. This phrase, which may well stand isolated in the context of indeterminacy, will lack nothing that is achievable of realizing the virtue intended by the traditional technique. It is a touchstone. The occasion of so sudden a flight may be simple nostalgia, looking backward.

But also it may be a reluctant testimony to real ontological efficacy, very much as it has been arrived at in the past experience of the race with its language; and to the impatience of spirited modern youth who will probably come eventually to sobriety and to power.

An Address to Kenneth Burke (1942)

I HAVE READ SEVERAL TIMES the long title essay of Kenneth Burke's book *The Philosophy of Literary Form,*[1] and still with the sense of an adventure. It is like following the intrepid explorer who is making a path through the jungle. I indicate the range and density of the speculative field, which is poetic theory, and junglelike; and also the emancipation of Burke the explorer's mind from common academic restraints—especially from the overall cast of sobriety which he, in a cold tone, calls "neo-Aristotelian." If he suffers from a restraint, I should think it is a constitutional distaste against regarding poetic problems as philosophic ones. I suppose his feeling may be that poetry is something bright and dangerous, and philosophy is something laborious and arid, and you cannot talk about the one in the

[1] *The Philosophy of Literary Form* (Baton Rouge: Louisiana State University Press, 1941).

terms of the other without a disproportion, and breach of taste. Who would not understand that? Aesthetics has been the fumbling chapter of philosophy. But I believe the philosophers themselves undergo the worst fits of depression, and have to wait for courage to return before they can resume their remote speculations with the right passion.

A kind of discourse which is past the matter-of-fact competence of science to explain, falls to philosophy. I had come to think that poetry must accept this attribution, and philosophy must sharpen its tools.

Nevertheless, there are some streamlined modern "sciences" which might be persuaded to explain poetry without benefit of philosophy. Burke's procedure is to work them for all they are worth, both severally and jointly, and then to supplement them with an ingenious all-out critique of his own. He has a whole arsenal of strategies, like the German general staff, who are said to have whistling bombs if they like, and whose campaigns rest upon a highly technical and sustained opportunism.

He begins by considering the poet as a "medicine man," and the poem as the medicine by which he tries to heal or "encompass" his own difficult practical "situation." We recognize the language of anthropology. The poet is a "primitive," who tries to manage his affairs by religious rite and magic. Burke is wonderfully keen at sniffing out ritualistic vestiges in even a modern poetry—taboo, fetish, name-calling, and so on. I wish he would consider more, though he does consider the possibility that anthropologists may have put their own bright colors on the forms of primitive religion, and that primitive men are really as various, and therefore as intelligent, as we are. Paul Radin, who spent six years with the Winnebagos but perhaps is not an orthodox anthropologist, told me that the medicine men were not magicians but philosophers, much as we assume our own best priests to be. But if they really are magicians, how does our own nicer sort of religion originate? The anthropologists do not illuminate this topic, which is discontinuous from theirs. It is striking that Burke does not permit us to confuse *him* with medicine-man mentality; is he then patronizing his poets? He is generous, and after many motions as good as concedes that primitive magic need not have much to do with poetics.

He defines the poem next as being in part a "dream," that is, a work of the unconscious; and there we have the Freudian science. The poem is not what it seems, it is not even what the author thinks it is. Freud announced the following understanding, and so far as I know never recanted from it. A poem is a discreet tract of imagery made laboriously, but without any knowing why, by editing libidinous phantasies that were in substitution for an act forbidden by the censor; the poem as it stands being such an ecstatic innocent—so excited about gray skies and little birds for example—that it is nonsense, it is unmotivated, unless it trails a lurid private history behind it. But what if the innocence is real? And how can you show it is not? There are many images not derived from libidinous phantasies; they happen every few minutes, and why not in poetry? To protract and record an innocent image seems indeed a remarkable action, it seems to be the aesthetic occasion, provoking some sort of philosophy to remark upon it; but if you have no philosophy with which to remark you are being rather arbitrary in remarking that it must be an evidence of secret guilt. Freudians have a most literal and painful version of original sin, and bank fearlessly upon it. But Burke is one of the most intelligent of writers, and has graduated with honors out of so many schools of thought that their testimonies do not tip him over but counterbalance each other. He is not too disposed to lump the guilty poetry and the innocent together, and therefore to think the Freudian strategy will work every time.

Then there is always "social science." With Burke it might

be expected that this would have a "Marxist" or "class" complexion, and he is a master of Marxist "dialectic"—an analytic instrument which is acute and has made incriminating literary discoveries, as I know to my discomfiture. But he does not force it, and I wish other Marxists would learn from his moderation. Social science is much wider than Marxism. For Burke the social dimension in the poem embraces such things as "prayer" and its opposite, imprecation, on the understanding, I suppose, that what is not magical in religion is social and addressed to the poet's own community; it has a "confessional" element and an "incantatory" element, terms which are Burke's translations of Aristotle's catharsis and mimesis respectively and denote the smart way in which the poet manages to shift his own burdens onto the shoulders of society. The social aspect of the poem seems to me inflated under Burke's treatment. But this science too comes to the end of its string.

Burke is within his rights, and puts academic critics in his debt, when he turns these lively sciences upon poetry to see what they will discover. They have their powers of divination, and can find in poetry their own slightly shady materials if they are there. What they find is principally what, according to my feeling, had better not have been there. But Burke's own special approach is quite different, and worth them all put together.

He conceives of poetry as drama, whether completely realized or not. He conceives of drama as the way the poet submits some personal and limited version of the truth about a situation to its ordeal by "unending conversation," to its test of survival against competing versions. Now some poems, like *Othello,* are actual full-blown dramas; in them you can find the rights of the situation contested by the different characters in turn. You have "dialectic": it is the "social way" of obtaining the truth, or rather, since society can hardly be said to initiate anything, even a search for truth, it is the social way of correcting and refining the truth that a given character has propounded. And the competition is not merely theoretical among the cross-purposes; force, accident, the logic of events, put views to the empirical test, and if the characters do not survive to take this crucial evidence into account the spectators do, and are the wiser. And the best truth furnished by this elaborate testing may not be positive truth at all, but a critical or negative truth; for the practical disposition of the argument may be catastrophe. We may reach a terminus sufficiently "encompassing" and happy for all, or one that is only ironical and indecisive, or one that is tragic and fatal. All this is within the range of the meaning of drama.

I suppose one tends to resist good instruction, and at first I thought that Plato's dialogues, and not dramas in the technical sense, would serve as the perfect type of dialectic for Burke. But I had to observe that they lacked the evidence of the action, and the arbitrament of the event. Then I thought that prose drama would do it, and perhaps do it better than poetic drama, because it would not require that kind of incessant diversion from the argument which is basic in the poetic medium itself, and which I have been privately calling the poetic "texture." (I still venture to think so.) If the several characters are in earnest about encompassing the situation, each in the simple way that suits his own perspective, and the ways are to prove conflicting, and we are to arrive at the social solution which is the way of ways and the "perspective of perspectives," all that is serious business, and prose is the language for business. But further, extended units of literature fit Burke's dialectical purpose, but not small units; what will he make of the lyric? He considers that a Shakespeare will manage to have every sort of poetry in the plays, somewhere among the speeches. If the lyrical passages have a content not specifically taken up into the argument, and not replied to, I think he would say they could have been replied to, but in fact remain dialectically undeveloped. The independent lyrics that lie outside of formal drama are dramatic to the extent of having a "character" speaker and an imagined "setting" and "business." Lyric becomes then a bit of imperfectly realized drama, and his omnibus conception of poetry as drama has room for it. As it is the less realized, however, it must be inferior. Its truth, he says, is local and relative, and never receives the social correction which would make it "absolute." But I think its localism is exactly what makes it admired, and thought to be poetry in the strictest sense. And he has inverted the usage of relative and absolute. There is an absoluteness in lyric which is primordial, and that is what a poetic theory should make us see.

It is hard to escape the conclusion that Burke does not have a philosophy of poetry, or does not have the right one, or does not have the right one by him always. He and I have exchanged communications at a brisk rate about points of doctrine. But I should like to address to him a bigger argument now. I hardly care to say that I propose to "get back to the fundamentals," a locution that sounds smug and religiose, and may be irritating and dangerous; if I lose my fundamentals I lose my case. I prefer his language: for the sake of "perspective" and "drama" I will go back a long way to bring up the argument.

2

Ancient man like modern man had his biological needs; he met them by studying and exploiting his "environment" (the natural and the social) intelligently; and the routines through which he operated were his practical "sciences." As they improved, he prospered. But suddenly and dramatically—for it blazes up with that effect in Greek history—comes a great addition to this common sort of business. After science, or in between sciences, at that comfortable moment when practical life was going very well, came philosophy, the "love of wisdom." I wish the force of the Greek word were still apparent when we speak of philosophy—as when the Phi Beta Kappas convene to talk about the "liberal education" which, like themselves, is so useless, handsome, and not very philosophical. The "wisdom" in the Greek is not the same word as "science," yet it comes automatically provided with its own motivation. "Philosophy" is indeed a motor term: it is the drive, the passion, for a kind of knowledge which is not practical, and biologically is superfluous. In Greek writings it means that quite fully, and hundreds of times. It would indicate a great indulgence claimed by man by way of diversion from animal constitution, and even the possibility of overdoing it and interfering with animal functioning. But Greeks took their stand on this human right. They were too radical not to be opposed; and for example by those who facetiously styled themselves Sophists, not the lovers of wisdom but the Wise Boys themselves, and contended that there were no motives other than selfish ones, and no wisdom other than practical knowledge. Kenneth Burke, stubbornly researching for the formula by which the poet in his poem would be found "encompassing his own situation," is sophistical; though he could retort that I am playing a "rhetorical" trick in attributing to him a "charged" and pejorative adjective by way of impelling him to make his peace with philosophy, Phi Beta Kappa, and liberal education. But his heresy can be put as simply as that.

Now I would maintain that Greek philosophy represents only, so far as its reputable exponents are concerned, a First Moment of this wisdom, in which the philosophers advance to an impossible extreme in one direction and have to retreat; and that there is a Second Moment, in which philosophy looks boldly in the other direction although—so like the Greeks we are, or so Occidental and like us were the Greeks—its procedure has scarcely yet got a thorough and hearty expression. It is within Philosophy II, not Philosophy I, that we find all that is distinctive in poetry as compared with science, and in "liberal education" as other than the cult of science.

As to the forms of this disinterested wisdom that the Greeks pursued. They found themselves projecting science for its own sake, science as theory rather than practice; projecting it further than need required; then stopping to admire its range, which took it far beyond the senses, and the apodeictic necessity of its conclusions. They defined such extension of science as wisdom, and for such wisdom thanked the faculty of reason. They became fastidious. Practical science, even "natural science" in its whole or extended range, had a certain meanness in that it operated with materials of great concreteness or impurity, so that its conclusions were tainted with corresponding contingency. They proceeded to scorn natural science and seek for a pure science, dealing with proper materials, which would be completely determinate, and whose conclusions would follow by necessity. I am thinking of such figures as Pythagoras, the Eleatics, and Plato, though I am oversimplifying the story. And the forms of knowledge which seemed to answer best to this description were mathematics; logic, an incipient wisdom closely related to mathematics; and ethics. Now for a remark or two.

Logic is a near relation of mathematics; but ethics, in its philosophical form, is not unrelated. We recall how pre-eminent among the virtues in glory, for the Greeks, was Justice; it is the most mathematical one. Now ethics seems to deal at best with highly impure and contingent materials. But the ethics of the philosophers differed from the ethics of natural man, first, by forgetting to be selfish—a great shift in motive—and, second,

on the theoretical side, by defining Justice, and the other virtues for that matter, in terms of their function in a human society. Ethics becomes what the natural man, like the animals,
need not, in matter of fact, possess: a philosophy of society.
The mathematical style of this wisdom took hold, for example,
when you conceived your own good as being but one unit of
human good, and mathematically no better than the unit that
might fall to any other man. Many thinkers of sophistical habit
have undertaken to demonstrate that the good of the greatest
number is your own good in the long run, but the Greek philosophers did not wait upon the demonstration, and in my own
experience it is never, upon the critical occasion, coercive. You
are just, but it is simply because that is your "philosophy"; you
will not find a better reason. And such philosophy is held by
"social scientists" as a rule. But, as with other admirable forms
of wisdom that come under the First Moment, there is danger
in it. Kant, and the Golden Rule, simply envisage any common
good, like food or money, and expect us not to care whether it
comes to us or to our fellow man. That amounts to justice, the
community of goods, and the rule of mathematical indifference.
But that may be too elementary for an ambitious philosopher
of the First Moment, such as Plato, or Hegel; whereupon he
applies himself to building up some specially tidy or "ideal"
society, and suits the citizen to the society; then, instead of giving them the common goods as we know them, suits the goods
to the citizens.

As for the mathematics, and the logic. These were the wisdoms
that seemed to operate upon any materials, and to constitute a
knowledge of pure or absolute Being; as if no insubordinacy in
the materials could affect them. They deserve this distinction if
any wisdoms do. But we may look briefly at some difficulties
discovered there by the Greeks. If mathematical and logical existents were Being itself, other existents for dainty philosophers

were Non-Being, and they were many. Indeed, all natural objects must rate as Non-Being. For Once-Being was Always-Being, but every natural object was forever undergoing alteration. It had a dimension of time; and Zeno's Paradoxes, including the one about Achilles and the tortoise, do not exactly indicate their intention, but at least they seem to say that some school was contending that calculations involving time were beyond the reach of a cogent mathematics. The natural object was specious Being, or Appearance. At best it was Becoming, something approaching the formal state of Being. The mathematical or logical operation expects that its terms will stay constant long enough to be operated on; but they may or may not; natural objects are given to shifting the very values you assume as your constant. For a long time I was puzzled by the dogmatic refusal of Greek philosophers to admit any grade of existence between Being and Non-Being. But equally I was puzzled by the paramount importance of the tautological Law of Identity, A is A, among philosophers both Greek and modern. I now think the two points of doctrine come to the same thing, and express a scruple of logical method, and also a nervousness at the place where there is most excuse for it. Your A must not change while you are arguing about it; first define it, then watch it to see that the definition sticks; but what happens too easily is that the natural object you define as A, whose residuary property x goes far beyond the A quality of your definition, is going to let its qualities irrupt to the surface and spoil the A quality; and this can happen even when A refers to the innocent numerical property. (To illustrate. The operation succeeds; but the patient dies. Or, an animal couple has the numerical value of 2; but animals have such energetic substance beneath any single property that presently your 2 has become 3.) The problem of any applied logic comes to this: to find an actual material whose substantival or residuary nature will not interfere with the given or surface quality you are discoursing about. And to keep saying that the least alteration turns your A to Non-A, or, A is A is A is A, is either by way of improving the illusion that you really have and hold your A, or else a mnemonic notice warning you to keep watch on your A lest it revert before you know it to Non-A, which is its other, material, and evil self.

The Eleatics powerfully insist on the Unity and Indivisibility of their so-called Pure Being. The terms meant little to me till I came to the conclusion that Unity and Indivisibility were bad ways of saying: Homogeneity. They refer to the quality of the material, not to the variety of the forms imposed upon it. In mathematics you have an abundance of distinct forms in the most determinate relation to one another, but it is imperative that you have a homogeneous material to support them. Monistic materialism is the objective of Greek or First-Moment philosophy. And, in fact, a scientific construct in any man's actual science is like a little monistic system in that it premises the material beneath the generic property it is studying, and hopes to find there a neutrality or inertness on the part of all the other properties which will amount to an effective homogeneity. The famous principle of the "uniformity of nature" is the Eleatic principle of Unity and Indivisibility, and just about as far from being a precise locution. More precise perhaps would be a principle of the "effective homogeneity" of the material. But if this is better language, that does not stop it from representing the scientist's pious hope rather than his objective datum. There is little ground for it in strict theory; which would suggest, on the contrary, that an actual material is substantival in the complete sense, or has an infinite series of properties, and no operation can be safe which does not allow for the whole activity of its material. We must believe therefore that any scientific process or prediction is only a piece of pragmatic knowledge. It is rude, since its calculation cannot be more than

57

superficial, but it will have to do; we will use it as long as it works.

It works, up to some marginal point where it does not pay for itself, in all sorts of situations. Our Occidental mind has been fertile beyond the dreams of our Greek original in finding occasion for its useful or theoretical employment, with the consequence that there are hundreds of going sciences and others coming on all the time. Their method, whether here or there, is no doubt as good as it can be, and probably through all its technical employments remains logico-mathematical, and is unified and determinate enough. (It might warrant a great international Encyclopedia of Unified Science.) But with respect to their material relations to each other the sciences are haphazard and incommensurable, and their separateness is absolute. Where a group of them deal with the same natural objects, as often happens, it is with different faces of the objects, or different qualitative surfaces, and it is the natural restriction upon a science that it works upon one of the surfaces only. We know that what is "material" to one science is not what is "material" to another though both materials be found in the same objects.

Plato dallied with Eleaticism, and retreated. It required living on principle in a world of such docile materiality as could not be found to exist; the stuff was not there, and if you tried to manage with it you were "not there." He came to terms with the natural world. But within that he could express his kind of preference, and hold to an ideal. He could participate in nature through his senses, while on all possible occasions exercising his reason. He embraced an eschatology, as follows. The rational principle within him was a soul, sent down from the heaven of Pure Being by God to inhabit the sensual body; but it must continue in militant rational activity in order to return to its home after deliverance from the body. I wonder if that seems an amazing doctrine. There is an irony if it sounds too strange

58

for us; what then is to be said about certain dogmas of our own Christianity? In the beginning was the Logos. God is a spirit, and they that worship Him must worship Him in spirit and in truth. The heavenly mansion is a house not built with hands. Earthly treasures are perishable, but neither moth nor rust can corrupt treasures laid up in Heaven. In Heaven is neither marrying nor giving in marriage. The philosophical passion of the Eleatics and Plato, transferred from place to place and generation to generation by many hands, including the one that held the sword for Alexander, came all the way to Jesus and Paul; to mortify the body and the senses in honor of the immortal soul. But there are other and counter dogmas in Christianity. There are Humility and Nonresistance, and there is Love, at the farther pole from Greek ethics. In the hands of the single-minded practitioners, or zealots, these dogmas are likely to realize an anarchy rather than a society; we hear of "philosophical anarchists." Love would seem to defend every kind of natural existence, and to embrace the heterogeneous itself, which for Platonists is the root of evil; and nothing would be more repugnant to it than the attempt to make the beloved objects conform to some standard not their own. The fact is that Christianity is not mere Platonism but has a wealth of doctrine, and there is paradox in its catholicity. And just as the aggregate of all a wise man's many wisdoms though not systematic may be said to "be philosophy," it might be said of Christianity that it "is religion," without much qualification; so inclusive it is.

Aristotle retreated a little further, but always, I think, with a characteristic ambiguity. God remains technically transcendent, and out of nature, but no longer claims a material substance; he is logico-mathematics itself, pure form, and in the sense that this is the ideal toward which the rational processes of man or nature seem to aspire he is the Prime Mover. No eschatology survives to lead to him the souls of the blessed, as if passing from one realm of substance to another. The rational soul has a sort of survival in Aristotle's system, but it is confused with the notion of the soul as entelechy, the principle of organization of the animal body; a principle which tries to keep the heterogeneous substance and the rational form going at the same time. (It is Hegel who makes most of organic form. The animal entelechy is the most brilliant thing in nature, seducing us into the wildest hopes, if we are looking for the power of rational form to dominate natural material on a great and compound scale. But, "by volume" as the chemists say, not much material submits to this fate; and the original materiality still greatly impedes the intelligent animal purposes; and the very best animal dies, as if to intimate that the materials had not been thoroughly converted.) Aristotle's interest is in this world, which under his analysis reveals more powerful determinations and promises than might have been expected by the skeptic. He is kin to the modern naturalists. His bias is toward realistic classification, and the discovery and generation of rational purposes that will actually do work. I am used to regarding this as according to the naturalist program, and naturalism as a kind of critical (or even "realistic") idealism. Perhaps this shows best in Aristotle in the way he likes to look at matter: as a stuff that is meaningless, as good as nonexistent, unless regarded as the "potential" of a new determinate existent under a form; and he pictures it as so amenable to the discipline of reason that it desires its own determination, and almost runs to obtain the form that is waiting for it. This view would pass easily into a doctrine of natural evolution and progress, and give us a world pulling itself up by its own bootstraps, which also might be congenial with the sanguine modern naturalists. But he finds this tendency balanced by an equal tendency on the part of the formed objects to disintegrate and revert again to mere matter.

His Platonistic speculations are bold enough, but he hedges, and saves himself by counterspeculations.

3

This sort of philosophy, ontology, or—religion, if it has anthropomorphic expression, or some animated metaphorical expression—is just as daring in its faith as experience and critical discretion allow. But it means work as well as faith, and suits the temperament that is fond of scientific and social programs. They seem to grow more daring as the faith retreats, the faith and the works coming closer together; the Kingdom of God on Earth, in Christian phrase.

A philosophy of the Second Moment (ambitious locution) if it is going to amount to something should be better than merely this first philosophy in retreat. It should have character of its own, and an attachment for something positive, ontologically "given" and assured. But I will not argue what it should be, for the Second Moment can be presented empirically.

It is the aesthetic philosophy; and as the other philosophy takes its bearings from the data of science, this takes its bearing from the data of art. The art is analogous to the theoretical science, as a sort of creative projection beyond the limits of the practical occasion; for natural man has no more use for art than for such a science. And if determinate form is what the science wants, what the art wants is the stubborn substance against which science breaks its head. Heterogeneous substance was conceded by Greek philosophers in accounting for nature's resistance to scientific process, but in art the heterogeneous substance is embraced. And in aesthetic philosophy, with critical self-consciousness. Though I should not suppose the philosophers would embrace it more warmly than the artists, at least they would draw up its bill of ontological rights, and locate it in the perspective. But it is embarrassing to have to think that Schopenhauer, Nietzsche, Bergson, Croce, who have the temperament for it, have not done this so precisely as did Kant, and possibly Aristotle, whose sympathies were not fully engaged.

Aristotle says, in the tone of commonplace, that poetry is chiefly an "imitation" or recording of natural objects in their concrete substantiality; or more probably of fictitious objects, provided these are on the order of natural objects and not too much idealized. Plato had said precisely this but in a scornful tone; accordingly he had almost abandoned poetry as too scandalous for approval. But Aristotle actually adds a redeeming or Platonic qualification: an imitation with a specially devised formal character, namely, phonetic organization or rhythm, as if to furnish a sort of "token" rationality for rational men. But he knows that poetic process is radically different from scientific. In science you "improve on" nature, in that you play up the form and play down the substantival matter, those two elements which, we can scarcely doubt, are equal in the sight of nature and of its ontological "principle." If then, after science, and knowing what science can do as well as what it cannot do, you choose to employ yourself with something described as "imitation," the rendering of the mere backward natural objects, you can only be intending to play up what you have been playing down: the matter. Aristotle remarks that we seem to have a propensity for imitation as well as for rhythm, and that imitation is a means of "learning" something.

Quite independently, Kant makes almost this identical analysis. In art we bridge the feud between those omnipresent faculties, sense and reason. We set up an object in which imagination —that synthetic faculty focusing all the senses at once—finds a complete heterogeneous image, and reason finds a definitive rational form, so that both can take their exercise in the same object. (A big and loose sort of object it should be, with plenty of room in it.) I do not think this understanding of art can be much bettered for introductory purposes. It can be elaborated. From Kant the imitationist, representationist, or "naturalistic" aesthetic, that likes to contemplate the most actual objects, can take its charter; but no more than "formalistic" aesthetics can, with its dogmatic liking for rational patterns. In poetry, the one dwells on the concrete "meaning," the other on the determinate meters.[1]

I will not go much further. But Kenneth Burke, for me, seems to be mostly in what I call the First Moment of philosophy, identifying himself with the scientific movements; which is very well, and any representations of mine against it would be impertinent, and as a matter of fact Kant is somewhere there too, and Burke knows his Kant. Burke has a theory of poetry, however, and Kant has a general aesthetic, and I wish to develop two or three considerations briefly out of Kant and address them to Burke.

And first, I do not think that Kant would go with Burke in his persistent effort to find in a poem the pursuit of some sort of useful or selfish "truth," or even some sort of dialectical or social "truth." Burke knows, we may be sure, that Kant carefully disengaged the artistic motive from "pleasure" in the common sense; then from "usefulness," which would involve it in a labor for the sake of pleasure; then from the pursuit of the ethical good and "determinate concepts," which together might

[1] It is more complicated than that, of course. In the matter of the meaning there is the rational structure organizing the surface by which the natural object immediately confronts us, and beyond that the rich concrete texture that discovers itself more gradually. In the matter of the meters there is both the structural regularity and the textural variation. I have written elsewhere of this.

be said to be wisdom itself, but wisdom of the First Moment. Art is radically not science, and not affiliated with the idealistic philosophy, and Kant does everything possible to prevent the confusion. The fact that Burke tends to confuse them might be an evidence that art is not really so "universal" a human activity as science; the "inside knowledge" of it is not so common. I agree that you cannot argue from your inside knowledge. I have been expecting to find somebody writing that Burke seems resolved to read into the poem everything possible along the lines of his own strenuous rationality and very little of the thing that makes the poem poetic; but that would get nowhere; the writer would be pitting his inside knowledge against Burke's. Kant has argued the motive business to the satisfaction of most aestheticians, in cold blood. To extend the Kantian terms a little, I think the trouble with Burke's readings is that his imagination plays too near the rational surface of the poem, and the reason it does not go deeper is that he is no lover of nature. In the last resort we shall not be talking intelligently about art unless we can pronounce with warmth two terms that must have been odious to a proper Greek: Love and Nature. (I am talking "poetically" now; Burke might say "too poetically.")

Next, we should be on our guard against attributing too much virtue to the "harmonious exercise" in the same poem of imagination and reason. It is splendid of art to have these old fighters making up. But I think it consists in their agreeing to take turnabout with the object, while disagreeing as hopelessly as ever as to what they want the object for. I read respected authors, and I have friends, who seem to me to misplace, and bring up on the wrong occasions, their admiration for harmony, and for such adjunct excellences as reconciliation, resolution, synthesis, unification, and plain unity. They are idealists, and suppose that the artists must share their idealism, it is such a good thing. But in the nature of the case this is impossible. In a scientific process there is harmony in the way the extended parts fit themselves spatially and temporally together, and the way each does its little bit of work for the whole and does nothing on its own account; which is unity, logico-mathematical harmony. But no harmony exists logico-mathematically among the heterogeneous properties of a natural object. You can compose separate apples into a nice total weight or volume or quota or money value or geometrical row or Christmas design of apples, but how can you compose a red and a sweet and a round and a heavy into one apple? To assemble the original properties is the work of nature, and the assemblage, if we think about it, always strikes us as arbitrary and contingent, a pure gift or datum, which reason cannot understand though sense witnesses it indubitably. The image is one thing, and the rational structure is another thing. The difference between the heterogeneous properties is absolute. Absolute also is the difference between the local imagery of the poem and its logical structure. Their being furnished both comfortably in one poem is a strange coincidence.

Finally, Kant sees the harmony of sense and reason broken in one instance, and reason triumphant most Platonically over sense. The occasion comes when art, or nature itself, manifests sublimity. The natural object exhibits vast magnitude, like the mountain (the mathematically sublime), or stupendous force, like the storm (the dynamically sublime). Both are of suprasensible dimensions, and imagination cannot take in the object as a whole to form a single image. It trails vainly in the wake of reason, which grasps the object easily. At first the disproportion between the cognitive faculties feels painful, but presently we are supposed to be comforted by the following reflection: the mind must have a supersensible destination; and we should be glad to abandon weak sense in honor of the rationality in store for us. I am obliged to think this comes to a vulgarization of Platonism (I hasten to say I find nothing like it in Burke), since Plato admired the purity or precision of rational form rather than its possible dimensions. In any case the size of the sublime object does not alter the force of the common Greek objection: you could not enter into your supersensible destiny without leaving behind you the sense-property that made your mountain a mountain and your storm a storm. Religions on the cosmic side are perfectly familiar with this crisis, and Kant himself declared, "A concept without a percept is empty." But I am interested in thinking of a possible reversal of the situation, and a "qualitative" or "substantival" sort of sublime. Sense has a fabulous realm to retire to beyond the reach of reason, if it wants to be so bold, a realm in which a chaotic qualitative density obtains. Matter would be its name. But if Form is empty, Matter is blind: "A percept without a concept is blind," as Kant, again, had said. The moral would be that artists can be just as fantastic as rationalists can. Artists have sometimes tried, not exactly to "purify" their art, which might imply the opposite intention, but to "densify" it, to the point where it may achieve emancipation from the bondage of any determinate form. The art feels wonderfully rich and strange to us then, and we strain ever so painfully to receive it; an adventure with boundless materiality. There is no passionate lover of his art who has not attempted it. But it eludes us. It is clear that imagination and reason ought to learn from the failures of each other's tours de force, and agree to inhabit their common and actual world. We cannot think that Kant found it profitable to sanction a single breach in their easy artistic "harmony."

4

These prolegomena have run beyond bounds, and it embarrasses me to think how many of them must already have been commonplace in Burke's own consciousness. But I can turn back to his view of poetry as "dialectic" with one of the biggest possible perspectives.

There are two kinds of poetry (or at least of "literature"), and Burke analyzes one kind with great nicety, and honors it, but shows too little interest in the other. The one he honors is the dialectical or critical kind, and the one he neglects is the lyrical or radical kind. But they correlate respectively (a) with the logico-mathematical ontology in retreat, and (b) with the ontology that is positively substantival or aesthetic. If one does not like "ontology" in this connection, then they correlate with two elemental "outlooks" or "world views," or for that matter with two religions, or two moralities, or even two kinds of politics. And of course they correlate respectively with (a) the temperament that cannot quite abandon its scientific orientation, and (b) the temperament which is capable of taking its art straight.[2]

I concede that the dialectic, which Burke equates with poetry, originates in at least a momentary disaffection with idealistic programs. It originates within a dissident, a critic, a skeptic, anybody short of an out-and-out cynic—names which describe a man with a negative attitude. But, in not being quite a cynic, he probably purposes with all his heart after being negative to be positive again; to be helpful. The dialectic entrusted to the characters (and the events) in the drama, who gradually reduce and refine the initial crude "truth" about the situation,

[2] If there had been time I think I would have proposed, instead of my rather blank and undescriptive First Moment and Second Moment, two exciting terms taken from politics: *Leftist,* for the logico-mathematical or Platonic or idealistic philosophy, involving the ontology and the religion and the ethics as well as the politics which that term connotes; and *Rightist,* for the substantival or aesthetic ontology, religion, ethics, and politics. These terms would have involved a long discussion. But I believe firmly in the method of philosophical correlations. It might yield us a real definition of temperaments; one more binding than, for example, Jung's introvert and extravert.

till at last they get something workable again, is too much like the consultation of the engineers, who have never really stopped intending to put their project through.

Of course the dialectical work is intelligent. I admire it, and I concede that it is intelligent in the degree that it works with more of the substantival object than the original fond idealist did. What it shows him is, in fact, how the properties which he was in too great a hurry to attend to will assert themselves nevertheless, and will amount to antistructures throttling his structures. For we do not tell enough if we say that the dialectic simply protests that he is being "too idealistic." So we have in the dialectical literature the familiar "tragic flaw" in the hero's character, which seems to make him the victim of his own virtues; the ironic turn of events that was foreseeable but unforeseen in the very "circumstances" that made the situation look most propitious; and, a still more startling kind of irony, found even within the restricted range of the lyric and pointed out to us by I. A. Richards, the romantic version of situation which goes to the trouble of accompanying itself with its own "parody," or antiromantic version of the situation, in order to anticipate the parody of the stranger-critic. All such turns are worked out in this literature with great specificity and with actual objects for illustration. But the original idealist himself had some image of the object. And the trouble with the dialecticist is that no more than the idealist need he have any patience with the residuary body of the image when he has done with it. The residuary body, with its irrelevance, is what constitutes the "free image." The poet embraces that but not the idealist, naïve or critical.

Not, at least, unless the critical idealist who writes plays has within his compound personality, as is quite possible, a poet also. I concede Shakespeare. Naturally I could have no argument with Burke as to Shakespeare's being a great poet as well as a dramatist. But I should try to distinguish the poetic effects from the dialectical ones, and defend the more isolated lyrical passages from any necessity of taking part in the strenuous dialectics. No more comfortable literary type will suggest itself to the Kantian than the big play, with its room for a long and keen work of dialectics or dramatics proper, and also for nearly incessant poetic effects. In general, I feel that the keener and more exacting the dramatics, the less energy there is for the poetry. But I think everybody knows that, and also the corollary proposition, that the imagery tends to be denser and freer in the independent lyric because the logic tends there to be simpler and more commonplace. The conclusion might very well be that the best dialectical or "true" drama comes in prose, the best poetry in the short lyric. And what could that mean but that you simply do not identify the dialectical and the poetical as a single "literary" element?

If there is not a regular and fairly technicalized provision for imagery throughout a body of literature, it should not be estimated as a poetry; and I would go further and raise the question whether it is entitled to be called even a "literature," or whether it is not merely a work of logico-mathematical process, which has every right in the world to use the dialectic in its own business; and I would raise the question at the expense of writings that superficially are fiction, drama, and even verse. I know that men of letters who are most jealous for their art can be very derisive against the notion that some weakly imagined work should have "literary" rating. They can be fierce, and I like them for it.

I will conclude by citing two technical evidences of substantival or poetic process in literature—without meaning that they are the only evidences. One consists in the "figures" or tropes. If we had an adequate "logic of poetic figure" it would be an anomaly, and would mean: "a logic of logical aberra-

69

tions; applicable to the conventions of poetic language." The tropes make departures from the logico-mathematical level of procedure, normal to prose writing, into substantival imagery, and that is their intention as poetry; at any rate the spectacular tropes do it, and so I have supposed do they all. But there is such a large conventional body of figurative usages, and so much writing in the way of merely halfhearted and verbal borrowing, making use of somebody else's descent into substance, that we have to be on guard against superficial evidence. The test would be one of pure logical analysis, or perhaps "semantics," employed by somebody experienced enough to detect the spurious or echoed old thing from the really new thing.

The other evidence would consist in some variety of "humor." I feel less sure about this evidence, which may require rather subtle interpretation. But I cannot help thinking that laughter is one of the profoundest of human actions, betokening ontological sense, and, specifically, that of the substantival existents as opposed to the better-advertised rational forms. I remember being taught that the definition of man as "risible animal" was enough to mark him off from the lower species, and that "risible" came to the same thing as "sapiens" or wise. Bergson's view of laughter is satisfactory enough; we laugh when we are invited to determine a human action by mechanical principles. We should add that the invitation is extended by somebody possessed of logico-mathematical mentality, and that our laughing is at his expense, and at our own to the extent only that we were nearly taken in. So we have satire, where a little touching up, a little more of the same, makes the program of the ingenuous idealist appear too obviously ridiculous; wit, including puns, indicating the inattentive colleague who does not respect the seriousness of the discourse, and broadening out into farce, and obstructive diversion and horseplay; irony, perhaps the subtlest of all, sensing that the simpleton idealist does not know he is handling dynamite and will be hoisted with his own petard. I am putting the grim interpretation upon humor. Like the dialectic, it is critical of programs. But not "constructively," to make them workable; nor does it try to furnish the frail logico-mathematical structure with some decent imagery in order to make it "ontologically" presentable. It sweeps the whole thing away with laughter; which, though wise, is primitive and organic rather than vocal, but, if it could be articulate, would be found reiterating, Substance, Substance. Humor is neither poetic nor antipoetic but prepoetic. The ambitious determinant is absurd by the same considerations that mark the substantival poem as beautiful.

However, I strongly advise not to sell Burke's poetics short. For he employs both figures and turns of humor, and his prose has literary distinction. Furthermore, he has written wisely, and in advance of the rest of us, about the logic of the figures, and some other purely poetic usages, to indicate participation in a true aesthetic. But this part of his thinking hardly shows in the work to which he has given the major title of *Philosophy of Literary Form.* He is perspicuous and brilliantly original, and I would venture to quarrel with no positive finding that he makes, but only with his proportions, or his perspective.

Positive and Near-Positive Aesthetics (1943)

I DON'T SO VERY MUCH MIND BEING CHIDED by Miss Hersch-berger for not speaking handsomely enough about poetry.[1] In the remarks of mine to which she refers I was anxious to learn and practice what has been hard for me in writing about poetry, namely, a temperance, and a reasonableness; I thought effort should be made to overcome the horrid barriers to communication between the factions. I felt prepared to furnish a usual show of zeal at some other time, as occasion might require. Evidently I seemed backward in this quality; but it is nice to be outdone in it by a critic so closely affiliated with the modern philosophies. Miss Herschberger is a graduate of the University of Chicago, evidently specializing in literature, and accomplished in the style of her critical prose.

[1] Ruth Herschberger, "The Structure of Metaphor," *The Kenyon Review,* Vol. V, No. 3 (Summer, 1943).

Apparently outdone. The positivists, according to Miss Herschberger, are anxious to recall their original famous doctrine that poetry emotionally might be "expressive," but semantically was "nonsense." But the way to win them to poetry now, in her view, is to show that poetry makes a very positive sense indeed. Accordingly she accepts the obvious prose argument at the center, and even considers that the "multiplicity" of items on the side (in the metaphor for example) really "integrates" into another argument which is "complete with usefulness, logical necessity, and true and reliable statements." This is to convert poetry altogether into prose, and to contend that its radical departures from prose are only illusory.

Now I scarcely detect a heroism in addressing the fierce positivists with a story of that sort. My own way of addressing them was to argue that the poetic texture was poetic and, irremediably, not positive; but that it attached itself technically to a positive center which it did not destroy. This seems to Miss Herschberger too "apologetic" and "political" a piece of tactics, which positivists will scorn. However that may be, will she not agree with me that the truth of our representations matters more than our salesmanship? If it takes too much guile to sell poetry over the notorious resistance of positivists, the salesman, whether she or I, might conceivably renounce his markets in that quarter; might we not?

Certainly there is a way of construing poetry as a discourse which is either scientific or something very like it and just as good; the idea being to find a very tidy logical unity in it, under the prepossession that a discourse must have this in order to be reputable. Those who construe in this manner, though I hardly think Miss Herschberger is one of them, practice what I should like to call a wishful positivism. They say to themselves: "There must be in this poem a decent integration, or unity, or logical organization, and also a decent objectivity, or verifiability, for we could not love it so much if there were not." In operation they may note that a poem does not feel a bit like a work of science at first, but they stay with it, and find in it a general argument, and under the argument some startling items that are hard to manage, until they begin to note that there are surely relations among these items, and to consider that when they talk about relations they are using more and more the language of science, whereupon they pursue the talking piously, till finally they are able to conclude that if their poem is not good science they are very much mistaken. Miss Herschberger thinks we should "refuse to admit for a moment" that metaphor brings any distraction, "over-particularization," irrelevance, or like disreputable importation, into poetic discourse. (I wish she would admit it for a moment, and actually feel it out, experimentally and fairly; to see if the world would stop turning under the odd condition.) But we must admire the stern conscience of the old positivism, which knew professionally the objectivity and logic that were in science, and declared as to poetry: "Here they do not appear." I think they were right as to the logic, and no luck can come to the effort to attribute to poetry all the syntactical qualities which belong to science. In my recent remarks to which her essay refers[2] I was deprecating Mr. Warren's argument, which seemed to be to the effect that poetry achieved a systematic interrelationship of all its compoments and was as neat and close a job as it could logically be: I felt that he was on the way to arguing that poetry is science, and even to being a positivist, insofar as he required that assurance in order to accept poetry. The Aristotelians at the University of Chicago, to whom Miss Herschberger devotes one of her most acute pages, would seem from her account to be far on the

[2] "The Inorganic Muses," *The Kenyon Review,* Vol. V, No. 2 (Spring, 1943).

way to the same destination; without knowing them so well as she does, I had observed how they professed a unique predilection for the poem's particularity, while in their analysis they tended to universalize it and smooth it out. Miss Herschberger herself desiderates science like a positivist, as I imagine, and may be somewhat indoctrinated in the "one and only" way of knowing. Her heresy is in hoping to assimilate poetry into science instead of giving it up as a bad job after the accepted fashion of the school. But she is sensitive to the poetic features which resist assimilation, and concedes that "science is admittedly inadequate at the present time" to analyze them in the sense desired.

But clearly there is a nonpositivist way to construe poetry. It would accept the analysis which science "at the present time" makes of poetic discourse because that seems obvious and just. The general consequence is as follows: A poem is a discourse in the sense that it has enough of a valid or scientific argument to hold it fairly together in spite of everything, with a sort of rough logical rigor, but it is everywhere particularizing itself, repudiating its nice abstract precision, and densifying itself with content which is not relevant to the argument. That, as I have contended, is evidently a "natural" though wayward thing for it to do in human hands. It seems to reflect a kind of ontological principle, or "reality principle"; it is about the dense, actual world which so easily escapes the net of pure science, utility, and efficiency, and, if we note it nevertheless, makes such a scandal of our Positive complacency.

In my opinion, there are at least three general human behaviors which it exceeds the canons of historic positivism to take account of, and which figure in our standard public life almost as prominently as science does. They are religion, art (including poetry), and philosophy; all of them superfluous if we wish them so, or going beyond use and function, in the

75

prodigality of the content they bring under attention. Their ontological interest is different from that of science though it may be just as genuine. And they may be sensitive or "knowing" though their cognitions are not a copy of those of science.

Poetry would seem to exercise our proclivity for a dangerous kind of knowledge; indeed, just as dangerous as M. Maritain represented in these pages last year.[3] It disregards the vital pragmatic economy and explores reality beyond the possibility of usefulness. To manifest a little of the zeal which I held back on the last occasion, I should say that this must be the knowledge which gods would practice, and it would be a far freer activity than the "geometrizing" which Aristotle imputed to deity. But for human beings it is such a dangerous activity that there should be restraints upon it, and are. We do not plunge into the maze of things without securing our retreat. Hence the rule that the poem never quite abandons the firm thread of its argument. It is not a poem at all without its free poetic "texture," of course; but its "texture" is incidental to its main "structure," which is scientific; so that I should have to concede that the poem is really achieved under the patronage, or perhaps we should say the unwilling auspices, of a scientific discourse.

When Miss Herschberger argues that the phonetic effects of poetic language are ancillary to the meaning, and reinforce it, she is in a hoary but, I think, minor and rather mistaken tradition. Using the lines of Shakespeare's *Coriolanus*,

> Murdering Impossibility, to make
> What cannot be, slight work,

she finds

[3] Jacques Maritain, "Poetry's Dark Night," *The Kenyon Review*, Vol. IV, No. 2 (Spring, 1942).

. . . a lucky opportunity to demonstrate that what appear as *sound* factors definitely contribute to the semantical import of a poem. Thus the brief and simple phrase "slight work" comes after a heavy and mountainous series of words, whose sound, accent, and meaning go to promote that mountain of Impossibility; when "slight work" comes, the breath-taking drop to such a simple discharge of "work" as these two syllables make it, is good theatre and reinforces the larger argument.

I should think that every bit of this analysis is founded on wishful positivism. I cannot find the mountainous series of words; nor in the "slight work" a sound-effect which describes either the "breath-taking" drop after going over a mountain, or the "simple discharge" of labor. We know what "slight" means, but its mere sound would never suggest that. "Slight work" is as heavy-sounding as "tight work" or "great work" and heavier than "life work." But it is always easy to oppose this argument-from-the-sound, dear to scores of critics far less gifted than Miss Herschberger, by making little verbal shifts and getting totally different results. Let us imagine the topic is how to conserve the produce of Victory Gardens, and re-write the passage this way:

> Furthering the possibility, toma-
> to canning-bees might work.

Given Miss Herschberger's descriptive values for the vocables, which would not seem fatally dislocated in the new version, how would she reintegrate them with the new meaning? I am compelled to believe that the sound-effects to which she calls attention are remarkable but do not "promote" any particular meaning at all. What is really remarkable in the sound is the iambic rhythm and the words' incessant but never successful effort to escape into freedom. It produces a music, low-grade

77

perhaps, insistent, compelling the sensitive ear's attention; inevitably at some expense to the argument. That is one of the side processes commonly carried on in poetry, and I do not know what a positivist can make of it on his usual principles. The iambic music of the speaker has about as little to do with his argument as has the color of his eyes. Its artistic value, indeed, is to produce the heterogeneous and not the homogeneous effect.

The poetic feature upon which Miss Herschberger's argument is focused is metaphor. I cite the illustration contained in her footnote because it is the simplest one. There she raises the question whether in an argument about "wildness" the metaphor "wild as a tiger" invokes the irrelevant fact of the tiger's stripes as well as the wildness. She says:

> I do not believe that stripes would have to be abstract and visual, but rather an integral part of the nervous, tense image of a tiger's body, hence contributive to the chief argument, "wildness." The wildness of a tiger, stripes and all, will differ from the wildness of a lion, that more ponderous, bearded fellow. Any referent truly *distracting* will be a fault in a poem.

But I am ever so happy to say that I have nothing to fuss about further. There would not seem to be any harm in being conscious of the tiger's stripes (and lion's beard) as part of the "wildness" of the beast (or beasts). But Miss Herschberger has already said that there must not be anything really distracting in our feeling for the images, and upsetting the argument we are pursuing.

For the argument is nothing less than the logic of the occasion, and it must be respected and brought to its proper conclusion. It is not so strict as the mathematical logic of science or the mechanical logic of technology. It is the account of some memorable play of our feelings and fancies, argued until it is fully finished; a true exercise of logic though it will be ideal or aesthetic, not factual and utilitarian. Miss Herschberger knows the experience so well that she is dedicated to the salvation of all that is positive in it, no matter how indefinite it may seem to the hardheaded mathematician or physicist.

Without such forms and exercises going through our heads we are deficient instances of humanity; perhaps superior in physics, or in trade and materialism; but children and innocents in aesthetic experience.

Art Needs a Little Separating (1944)

MR. AMES HAS GIVEN ME PERMISSION to follow him with some comment upon the general state of aesthetic studies, in the light of his essay.[1] It seems to me an essay which does throw light upon contemporary discussion, and is important for that reason as well as in itself. It is one of the politest of essays, and seems generous in its attributions to art. Nevertheless the kind of technical terms it uses is decisive, so that we say: It issues from that rugged philosophy of which everybody must have said to himself that the recognition of art will be the last thing it will do. The essay leads toward the recognition, and that is exhilarating.

Nearly every locution suggests the author's philosophical commitments: he is one of the tough moderns. In another

[1] Van Meter Ames, "Art and Science," *The Kenyon Review*, Vol. VI, No. 1 (Winter, 1944).

essay,[2] which he was good enough to show me, he began as follows:

> The great controversy in aesthetics hovers over the question whether art and the attitude appropriate to it are separated from other human interests and activities or intimately bound up with them.

It seemed to me that this dilemma might be more rhetorical than real, and its language charged in favor of the second alternative. For it is too likely that art is bound up with other activities in part, and radically separate from them in part. But from the above beginning his reader must have prepared to learn presently that art was bound up just about indistinguishably with the other activities, and that some aesthetic theory which had a separatist tendency was irresponsible and antisocial.

But it is better, when art begins to be extricated from its bonds, and distinguished. For Mr. Ames the departments of activity with which art is bound up chiefly are the scientific and social ones. This is according to that same dominating philosophy: a socioscientific way of thought which has been too compulsive upon its adherents, with terms of discourse which have been inflexible and chilling, like those we meet with, let us say, in the Roman Catholic philosophers. It is all the more remarkable if he finds that art does separate itself eventually from science. But I am sorry that he should not indicate how clean the breach is, and speculate upon its consequences. He does not play up sufficiently what he discovers; he leaves it almost obscured in the profusion of his social and scientific professions.

[2] "On Empathy," *Philosophical Journal* (September, 1943).

To review now the identity which art has with science, and then its difference.

[We commonly say that a work of art is a discourse, or piece of ordered language; that it makes statements and conducts an argument; or, if it is not literature, that at any rate it is a composition having logical relations among its parts.] In these terms we acknowledge the easy and obvious aspect of the art-work, if not the one which is remarkable to its devotees. If, now, we say that the work inculcates a moral value, it comes to much the same thing. It comes to science; for what is moral in the usual sense, that is, beneficial, is genuinely useful, is some instrument of reasoning which, on the technical side, is a work of science. The good and the true are not in opposition but in conjunction, or complementation. And science may well be the best general name of the one good work and true in which they combine.

Within science, there are excellent modern names for the single unit of constructive effort, the affective discourse which formulates something of moral value. One is "process." A similar one is "operation." The formal human career may be said to be a sequence of operations. But the key word by which Mr. Ames describes a discourse is Dewey's word, "hypothesis." A man is impelled to take action when he finds himself uncomfortable, or in need, or lost, in some given "situation"; and to try to deal advantageously with it in any fashion is to invent and work out a hypothesis. I am not quite sure of the terminological advantages of hypothesis over operation. Operation sounds a little more technical, and colder; actually the term is used often in mathematics. Hypothesis sounds more venturesome, and more dramatic, as well as more modest.

It is a broad term. It seems to cover the whole gamble of human behavior, as we feel our way into the natural environment along the possible and practicable lines. Mr. Ames, like Mr. Dewey, means it to cover works of art as well as works of science. And it does. Clearly a work of art carries a hypothesis about what nature is like, and what standard or causal sequences seem to obtain in our human reckoning of nature. In this sense the artwork is a utility, and its moral and technological values are eligible for discussion. Apologists do their art no service in seeking to exempt it of moral and scientific responsibility, and to have it out of the category of useful human behavior. Art, if it takes them at their word, falls into forms that seem to be all but void of human interest, as well as forms that are strange and all but unintelligible; the human quality has dropped out of it.

And how does art differ from science after having conformed with science? I condense into one passage some of the rather dispersed observations which Mr. Ames has about that. I believe I am stating the single sharp differentia which he assigns to art. In science the work originates in a given situation, which is presented to perception in all its confusion; but it "moves steadily away" from perceptions to "abstractions." Here hypothesis shakes itself free from irrelevant circumstance in order to be ready for further and professional business. But there is also hypothesis which works within the mesh of the profuse perceptual circumstance, and stays there. "The flights of art keep hovering about their sensuous base and keep being satisfied there." (How different it is from the hypothesis of regular science, whose destiny is to be transformed into a "universal" with no traces of the basic situation, and indeed with no visible perceptual situation at all.) The universal or scientific version of hypothesis points toward future use; the hypothesis that sticks at the aesthetic level does not look forward. Science "denatures experience," while art "endeavors to pluck elements of experience without seeming to uproot them." Summarily: the products of art cannot be understood "apart from a situational matrix."

The consequence of this differentiation, I should judge, is a bigger breach with science than Mr. Ames seems to acknowledge. Without the universal terms, and the professed job of setting up a rule or standard, the hypothesis can only be rude or embryonic science; adequate for bringing under control its single situation, but not negotiable, playing no part in the vast explicit organization of the world for human possession. On what ground does art care and dare to restrict the moral-scientific process, which is the human process, capable of completeness and dignity, to a half-conscious and primitive level? And I will put the corollary question. What is there to be left behind and *lost* if we choose to move on from this level into perfect science? Mr. Ames scarcely asks this question, whose significance for the human economy—like the future of poetry, which depends on it—is immense. He does say that art is "distinguished by the perceptual enjoyment of its material embodiment"; and he represents matured scientists, who have put behind them the perceptual enjoyment, as liking to go back and recover it. A long discussion suggests itself about two highly alternative attitudes to nature in the first place: the one which proposes to bring the natural situation into service, and the one which cherishes its "enchantment"; for Mr. Ames uses the last word too. But we cannot make much of his hedonistic expressions; they are not frequent, nor yet firm.

I think nevertheless that Mr. Ames has made a right start. "Situational matrix" and "hypothesis" may not look like the promising basis for a theory of art, but they are workable.

Yet I wish to try some of the older terms upon which aesthetic theories have been founded; I greatly need their help in focusing this discussion. Immediately I am embarrassed by a sense of impertinence toward Mr. Ames: in the consideration that he has an official place in the academy himself, and knows the classical aesthetic systems several times better than I do, who am only an amateur of philosophy, and yet he has not found it advantageous to cite them. It is characteristic of the modern philosophers to propose not to borrow from the old ones, and it is well known that they have started philosophy all over again, from the bottom up. In this essay of Mr. Ames's, appeal is not once taken to the authority of Plato or Aristotle, Kant or Hegel; we may judge that authority is not necessarily conceded now to these elder philosophers. I think that may be very well. When positivism repudiated "metaphysics" and formally initiated the new philosophy, it was, significantly, just after the old philosophy had committed itself mortally to rhetoric, a yearning and "weighted" terminology; scruple for the little fact was nearly gone from the vagaries of romantic German idealists, though the wordplay of Hegel went under the name of the "dialectical method." There must be grave doubt whether it is to the net advantage of young men to become Doctors of Philosophy at the cost of struggling through this material. The academic philosophers tend always to be too respectful. We know the locomotor ataxia that besets the earnest scholar as he responds to all the famous philosophers in series, and politely employs their own terms—which is to take the philosophers at their face value—in appraising them. As an alternative, I should very nearly as soon put faith in the pedestrian empiricism of the moderns, trusting them in time to take me all the way.

Let me make this profession of faith more carefully. I admire the moderns for the honesty and rigor of their analytical methods. On the constructive side, with their humanistic and pragmatic views, I think they have integrated the good and the true more tightly than philosophers have ever done before, referring these terms as they do respectively to the motor and the rational processes, the complementary aspects of human action. They have justified science by tying it up with common

85

moral impulse, and justified morality by putting it straight to work in science. But this is a binomial integration. The beautiful does not necessarily enter into it, and they have not yet done much about that, nor shown the disposition to do much. The very tightness which they have built into their integer disinclines them to admit the element of beauty, which will import a looseness.

Unqualified dedication to the type of human action—which is science—does not leave room for art. So I turn to Hegel, though not without a proper disrespect. Today we can hardly endure a certain complacency, or unctuousness, which we sense in Hegel, but it is my idea that Hegel's aesthetic views are subtantially the views which suit the modern position; and that, if Mr. Ames, with his provocative differentia for art, should find Hegel's views uncongenial, he must equally have a quarrel to make with the modern philosophy. Hegel is one of the begetters of this modernism. But with his terms we recover our sense of the real issues in aesthetic theory.

1. Hegel was of course a monist: the real is the rational. As for the discourse of art, either it is the work of rational spirit (*Geist*) or it is not, according to Hegel; and, according to the moderns, either art is science or it is not. If art is not an activity of *Geist,* or, indifferently, if art is not science, then it is an activity which philosophers need not be at pains to respect. But it was according to Hegel's sanguine temperament to reject as little as possible, and to represent art as conforming well enough with his own purposes. The moderns have been more realistic, and many have determined that art was not science, or not competent science, and scorned it. But doubtless as many, if they have pronounced upon it, have not differed substantially from Hegel; they have judged that art is science, and that it will do; an amiable and not very fatal position.

2. If truth and moral goodness reside in the work of *Geist,*

where is beauty? For Hegel fine art is the picture of *Geist* at work, performed in a useless "medium" like pigment, tones, words, for contemplation only. *Geist* steps back and looks at *Geist,* becomes self-conscious, meditates its own image. Man, says Hegel,

> has had the impulse to express himself, and so again to recognize himself in things that are at first simply presented to him as externally existent. He attains this end by altering external things and impressing on them the stamp of his own inner nature, so that he rediscovers his own character in them. Man does this in order that he may profit by his freedom to break down the stubborn indifference of the external world to himself, and may enjoy in the countenance of nature only an outward embodiment of himself.

It follows that art is the portrait of the artist; beauty is the warm suffusion that comes with the recognition of one's own likeness in unexpected places; and the name of this department of activity might well be narcissism. Are the moderns forced into the same construal of art? I believe so, though they may not be vain enough, or sophisticated enough, to assert it; and out of their own modesty they may dislike art, and reject it. Art is a useless *representation* of triumphant process, operation, or hypothesis, such as has already perfected itself in action and imposed its order upon nature. I will only remark that a little vainglory is scarcely worth attention, but a great deal of it is a sign of weakness, and morbid; and on this basis the arts had better have a small budget to operate on.

3. The whole philosophy of Hegel is concerned with confirming his rational monism, and therefore with assimilating the Many into the One, or sense into reason, or matter into form, or nature into the scheme of human values, and so on. This is also the problem of the modern thinkers, if their in-

terest in science is ambitious enough to project a speculative philosophy at all. But Hegel employs characteristically a literary sort of technique: the trick of paradox. The long sequence of steps in the ladder contains many paradoxes. The paradigm of them all is of the form:

> Thesis and Antithesis do not exclude one another but unite to produce Synthesis.

One would have said that it takes Thesis and Thesis to produce Synthesis, or Thesis A and Thesis B to produce Synthesis AB; whereas Thesis and Antithesis produce nothing at all when we try to join them together, or, to put it formally, produce Synthesis O. In literature it is common to find contradictories asserted, and that trick is teasing and smart; but there is no intent to deceive, and the intelligent reader is only led to look closer and discover that they are not really contradictories. When Shakespeare represents the union of the Phoenix and the Turtle, he insists for several quatrains upon the paradox of the two become one. Thus:

> So they lov'd, as love in twain
> Had the essence but in one;
> Two distincts, division none:
> Number's self in love was slain.

A very old conceit, but it was well phrased, and then several times rephrased without quite repeating itself. I have observed in other readers as well as myself a little uneasiness in feeling that Shakespeare was carrying his game too far, since the lovers certainly do not lose all of their respective identities, as we know very well when challenged here to look into it. I think there may have been in my mind the very idea that the luxurious Hegelians might read triumphant paradox from so apt a text; and certainly I have known Shakespeareans who believe in the literal inspiration of their master, and about this very poem tell us how serious it is, and how profound. Shakespeare had far too much good sense to be under any illusions as to what his commonplace paradox amounted to. It amounted to a long piece of conceit in the paradoxical kind, and was his exhibit in a book of literary exhibitionism. He had not put much of his poetic force into it, nor did he depend upon paradox for the staple of his real occasions. At least this is my supposition.

As for that, Hegel too had good sense, and made the most acute distinctions. But flat contradictions are much more adaptable to monistic treatment than acute distinctions, and the fiat of the paradoxes is Hegel's monistic display.

There are desperate problems of reconciliation which monistic rationalists must undertake, Hegelian or modern. The modern ones are extremely conscientious about respecting the isolated datum, the fact; and the critical fact for them is that any unit of material nature is a vast confusion of properties; the Leibnitzian *confusio,* or assemblage of perfectly factual and even "vivid" properties which make up concreteness, and render it eternally other than the "distinct" or selective object of reason. Among these properties many must remain irrelevant to any rational order that tries to express the concreteness, and they cannot be engaged by it. Paradox consists in saying anyway that they are engaged, and that the irrelevance is overcome. Nature and rational order are incommensurables. They are not truly antithetical, except to a monist, since nature does not exclude a great deal of order, and science is always a true account of nature as far as it goes. But monism is an extravagant affirmation, and it dramatizes nature as pure disorder, and reason as the champion who overcomes and redeems it.

4. The specific paradox upon which Hegel relied for handling the art object was: the *concrete universal.* Now we would

be quite prepared to hear about a *complex* universal. Let Hegel's favorite kind of universal be equated to the operation or the hypothesis of the moderns. The most complex one will be the finest one; a whole of discourse whose parts are extremely heterogeneous, and function dutifully but in unlike ways within its working. A machine is a complex universal; an animal organism in action is a better one; and the Binomial Theorem is perfect. But in none of these as a formulated universal does the complexity cover the Leibnitzian confusion that is present in the work of art. Hegel did not want to say confused universal, and he could not have originated so distinctive a philosophy by saying complex universal. Hence the gaudy paradox of concrete universal.

It is hardly necessary to convince the experienced analyst, or for that matter the experienced linguist, that concrete universal is not a valid locution. A true universal is an ideal operation in which partial and abstract functions contribute, but not parts with concreteness or material substance of their own; the private energy of these parts must overflow their functions. A universal can no more be formed out of concrete parts than is a concrete object formed out of abstract functions. In practice, the most that is expected on behalf of an operation is that the private energy of the parts—that of the chemical tissues of the animal body, or that of the metallic parts of the machine—will not impede their functional operations, but will remain inoperative, for a long time.

Hegel's concrete universal for the art-work has been in effect translated many times into modern language, though not very happily. The rich detail of a piece is said to be transmuted into the effective single design; or, what appears local and irrelevant is taken up into the higher relevancy; or, in all this heterogeneity there is no breach of the logical unity. To the literary sense paradox carries no deception, but believed in literally it is magic.

5. Very instructive is Hegel's eventual repudiation of art. His real passion was for such universals as the Theory of the State; they were pure *Geist,* he said, and "transcended" any work of art; they had sheer dimensions, and what was probably more important, they had a nicety of articulation, which exceeded anything that could be observed by the senses. But this reasoning is incomplete. The natural objects, or the representations of the natural objects, transcend the so-called concrete universals of pure *Geist* in the numerical heterogeneity or density of their concrete substances; and the match is even again. Hegel's concrete universal, which could not quite be sustained in the art-work because of the overflow of the concreteness, is retired to the domain of pure *Geist,* where the concreteness is a polite fiction, and the universal may luxuriate in its full range and precision, with parts to suit. Art becomes finally for Hegel the thing to educate boys with, or to put before the great herd of men of mediocre capacity; it is outgrown by them if they really mature in the power of *Geist.* It strikes us only too painfully that this attitude is prevalent among moderns too, who think that art is juvenile, or adolescent, and that in the right order of progression poetry gives way to prose. It is indeed true that science advances by leaving art behind. And no exception must be taken to this insofar as we have an interest in advancing science. But the consequence is to render science and art all the more disparate.

In this far too simplified review of Hegel's aesthetics I see I have made no reference to Mr. Ames's essay. But it has been increasingly on my mind. The Hegelian position is very close to the general one from which he must have started out. But we may imagine him disaffected at various points, and at Point

5 he diverges, or perhaps it would be better to say that he stays behind, in the "situational matrix," to keep company with the science which refuses to advance because it is fond of its aesthetic effects. He contends that hypothesis which does its work, though it never gets out of its situational matrix, is still genuine, and in its duty. I suggest that he must nevertheless acknowledge what a liability aesthetic experience means to the advancement of science. And he should consider how precarious its defense must be against the passionate humanism which is in modern science as much as it was in Hegel. He will need further and much more radical arguments by which to make this defense stand up.

Art Worries the Naturalists (1945)

Who in Turn Worry the Arts with Organism,

Fusion, Funding

THE APOLOGIST OF THE ARTS cannot do otherwise than refer
the question of their strange kind of activity to the current
philosophies; therefore, in these days, to naturalism. I have
some acquaintance with the writings of Dewey, especially *Experience and Nature,* and *Art as Experience;* with those of Santa-
yana, who is also a kind of naturalist, less patient and methodical
but more imaginative; and, as to the degree of my respect for
them, I do not hesitate to think that these are major figures, if
there are any, which our country has contributed to the world's
philosophy. They write at great and loving length about art
and the aesthetic experience. I know also the able little book,
Aesthetic Quality, by Professor Stephen Pepper, which employs naturalistic categories that Dewey had promulgated.

But it is a comfort for the mere literary man to feel that he
can speak of philosophical naturalism with some assurance

that he means the same thing by it as the general run of its adherents do. Consequently, I am grateful for *Naturalism and the Human Spirit,*[1] the new volumes of essays by fifteen different naturalists, including Professor Dewey himself. They are admirable deliverances, for example in the clarity of presentation, and avoidance of technical jargon, which are among the public characters of the school. One feels that naturalists are about as responsive to public opinion as it is to the public interest that they should be. And now, or at least here, they are conciliatory. There cannot often have been a new philosophy with as many urbane and reasonable expositors at once. If the most obvious enemies of the naturalists are the supernaturalists, these would do well to counsel earnestly as to the manners of their own polemic. If it seems impertinent in me to say this, let me remark that I have myself come down a long and rather absurd hill. Like my preceptors I used to regard naturalism as a specially malignant heresy, if not an abomination unto the Lord. But now I venture to think that even this quarrel is a verbal one, rather than an inarticulate feud of the blood, and that the issue needs most to be spread out in words and examined. If there is anywhere a philosophy indigenous to our local climate, it is naturalism; whereupon, even if America were not my country, I think I should not care to convict this philosophy of inherent viciousness, but at most of an immaturity. In the volume mentioned its own expositors still draw careful attention to its youthfulness.

Naturalism is chiefly, so far as I can see, a philosophy which rationalizes the protean activities of science as we in this age and place know them and engage in them; therefore a new philosophy, and indigenous. It must be said that logical positivism also is such a philosophy. But we can now see where

[1] Yervant H. Krikorian, ed., *Naturalism and the Human Spirit* (New York: Columbia University Press, 1944).

naturalism has gone decisively beyond positivism, and left to it what may be regarded as an intransigent minority position. Many of the present essayists are at pains to disclaim two misdemeanors which are still commonly and widely charged against them. They decline to commit the "reductive fallacy"; that is, to think the grand objective of science is the reduction of mind to matter, or the conversion of biology and even psychology into physics. At the most they claim that the physical data furnish "correlations" which might identify but could never describe the organic and conscious objects. And with equal firmness they refuse to commit the "genetic fallacy." As staunch evolutionists, they find in the lower forms the historical context from which the higher forms emerge, but not the figurations of the higher forms, nor in any substantial sense the prefigurations.

The naturalists are good at objective analysis. What they analyze is a wide variety of activities which, in their opinion, constitute human behavior. But they have to approach it with some method, which means with some prejudice; and theirs is the very plausible one to the effect that behavior is the way in which the species tries to master its natural environment for the sake of its vital or animal objectives, and that its success depends on the degree in which it employs the scientific technique. Their grand perspective of the types of masterful human action includes by all means the political and social ones; these are important actions, where the masterful creatures coöperate, and had better do it with any social science which may be available, to take the field together against resistant but yielding nature.

But it is right that we should call something to the attention of the naturalists; a behavior or two which appear rather different from these, with an outlook that does not deserve to be glozed. Sometimes the field does not seem to evoke from man the conquering action. It is as if some invincible residuum had asserted itself on nature's part, or else some scruple asserted itself in the conqueror. I have observed—unless in part I have only fancied—that a naturalist appears a little nervous, if he does not appear a little blank, when he encounters a concept of nature too big to categorize within the comfortable "non-ontological" procedures of science. This would require a sense of nature big enough to deploy the numerous action we call religion; or the one we call art; or for that matter the numerically still larger one which we might call sentimental attachment, this being for individual natural objects, or for persons and social objects, all of them apparently inviolable and respected in their own objective natures. In these kinds of behavior the object appears to us as a dense area of contingency, that is, a concretion, a reality on which we cannot take our usual firm grip, and a foreign if not unfriendly being. Toward this object the human creature assumes suddenly a new humility; it figures in religion as a sense of awe, in art as a sense of beauty, and in sentimental life as an uncritical affection. Nature as encountered in these objects does not seem to forbid him, nor even the aggressions he commonly practices upon it, and despite its Sphinxlike silence, and principle of prodigious exuberance which is so alien to human understanding, seems to receive him. I am afraid this is metaphorical language such as naturalists must abhor. Description of these experiences flows spontaneously into metaphor, which is rather as if it flowed into the sea, but is there no concept recoverable from the metaphors? Behind any religious formulation, I should guess that some religionists had wearied of trying to extricate the concept from the metaphors and simply adopted the nearest one. I am trying to identify, by way of advance notice at the top of this essay, a common kind of adaptation which we make to environment. If it is not imperative in the first place, as the belligerent survival-adaptation is, it is imperative in the second place, which is one of handsome dimensions. *Nihil alienum puto,* the naturalist says about the comprehensiveness of his choice of human experience. They should look to their reception of these specific experiences; these are commonplaces of human behavior, but the naturalists have not yet done them justice.

2

My title mentions organism, fusion, funding, as concepts under which naturalists dispose of art. And these are all in Dewey. But there is something else in Dewey which is absent from the writings of the younger naturalists: a tangle of bold philosophical speculations which are religious as well as aesthetic, and do not yield any firm or demonstrable results. I am prepared to think that speculations on this order are probably imperative, and incidental to the hazard of being human, though a working aesthetic theory may be had without them.

There is probably a "philosophical distance" between Mr. Dewey and his followers; in their writings the speculation is at a minimum, as if because he had speculated for them, vicariously and already. So, for example, they make little or no use of his "radical" kind of empiricism (to give it William James's adjective) though methodologically they are empirical. According to this doctrine, it is wrong to regard the familiar Cartesian dualism between subject and object (or man and nature), so harrowing to modern thinkers, as ultimate for philosophy. For subject and object are only inferences made in reflection from an original spontaneous experience which was integral, knowing neither subject nor object. Philosophy should deny the sufficiency of either of these disparates and return, in principle at least, to the integral experience. How shall philosophy in fact return? T. S. Eliot, in a poem, has rung the changes on the text, "Since I shall not return." Our age of innocence has gone. But Dewey holds that in aesthetic experience we actually make the return. He takes very little interest in mere "nature," in the picnic sense or the Wordsworthian sense, as objective landscape. It is only when this landscape and an artist's mind have interacted, and produced their joint "experience," that we have nature proper or nature absolute; it is identical with art, and it embodies man and environmental nature indistinguishably:

> But so to conceive nature [i.e., as excluding man] is to isolate environing conditions as the whole of nature and to exclude man from the scheme of things. The very existence of art as an objective phenomenon using natural materials and media is proof that nature signifies nothing less than the whole complex of the results of the interaction of man, with his memories and hopes, understanding and desire, with that world to which one-sided philosophy confines "nature."

But the difficulty of this argument almost forbids the use of it in a literary essay. First, the work of art is an "objective" record for the art-lover to appreciate, though in it there is said to be neither object nor subject; I see a chance that this may be so, for the art-work is exemplary, and contemplating it we may perhaps transcend our normal vision and know at last what nature in Dewey's absolute sense is really when, unaided, we should be blinded to it by our own imperious egoism; perhaps nothing stranger than having a perspective of ourselves having a perspective. But we go on, and presently are dismayed to reflect that the artist himself could never have had the absolute vision which his work has bestowed upon us; as pure subject he was busy acting upon nature (i.e., nature external and limited); and whatever nature may have contributed, his contribution was to enforce his stubborn memories, hopes, etc., upon nature, the act of a child or primitive or animal who was all subject going after his object; which does not square with our conception of the dignity of the artist. Finally, there remains the insoluble question of the mode of nature's participation in this interaction; for Dewey's idea is that of a perfectly reciprocal action; but a natural action analogous to the human action, and for instance a conscious natural action, takes us into the precarious realm of the supernatural.

Dewey is quick to react against the supernatural in the forms in which we ordinarily conceive it. For example:

> As to absorption of the aesthetic in nature, I cite a case duplicated in some measure in thousands of persons, but notable because expressed by an artist of the first order, W. H. Hudson. "I feel when I am out of sight of living, growing grass, and out of sound of birds' voices and all rural sounds, that I am not properly alive. . . ." The mystic aspect of acute aesthetic surrender, that renders it so akin as an experience to what religionists term ecstatic communion, is recalled by Hudson from his boyhood life. He is speaking of the effect the sight of acacia trees had upon him. "The loose feathery foliage on moonlight nights had a peculiar hoary aspect that made this tree seem more intensely alive than others, more conscious of me and of my presence. . . . Similar to a feeling a person would have if visited by a supernatural being if he was perfectly convinced that it was there in his presence, albeit silent and unseen, intently regarding him and divining every thought in his mind."

But immediately Dewey rejects the supernatural presence and remarks:

> I do not see any way of accounting for the multiplicity of experiences of this kind (something of the same quality being found in every spontaneous and uncoerced aesthetic response), except on the basis that there are stirred into activity resonances of dispositions acquired in primitive relationships of the living being to its surroundings, and irrecoverable in distinct or intellectual consciousness.

The supernatural object for Dewey is an atavism, or throwback to primitive mentality. But it seems fairly innocent of vicious consequences for the experient who elects this form of expression; a fictitious expression which focuses, or brings to one tangible head, a series of natural phenomena that is massive in the aggregate yet not homogeneous enough to be really added up. This object seems to Hudson as sensible of him as he of it, so that here is a really reciprocal situation in which the subject and object know and love one another; the condition to which the aesthetic experience in Dewey's view seems always to aspire. But the common language of religion and of love do not readily pass the lips of this homely Vermont thinker whose heart is so sound yet whose metaphysics must be so abstract, or we might say Protestantized.

In the volume of naturalist essays there is a sharp little passage in which Professor Thelma Z. Lavine takes Professor Dewey to task for his homage to preorganic nature, very much to the same effect as his chiding of Hudson. Dewey had written:

> To me human affairs, associative and personal, are projections, continuations, complications, of the nature which exists in the physical and pre-human world. There is no gulf, no two spheres of existence, no "bifurcation" . . . to anyone who

takes seriously the notion of thorough-going continuity. . . .

The idea of continuity is not self-explanatory But its meaning excludes complete rupture on one side and mere repetition of identities on the other . . . The growth and development of any living organism from seed to maturity illustrates the meaning of continuity.

Professor Lavine regards this as metaphorical language and rejoins:

To affirm the "growth" of the "higher" out of the "lower," to deny "gulfs," "gaps," or "breaks," is to speak the language of the seer, not of common sense or science.

Now we must have wondered what nature ought to mean to the organic individual who has emerged from the organic matrix without really, that is irretrievably, breaking the continuum. There is room for a theology here, to look out for a continuum which must be threatened by the slight rupture called birth. As God is said to have created man out of His own fullness in order that he might praise Him and aspire to be united again with Him, so it might be considered the highest role of Dewey's emergent man to overcome his own individuation and make himself one in consciousness, or it may be unconsciousness, with the matrix. (In Oriental religion, metaphysically far stiffer than the popular religions of the West, the career of the individual consciousness, separated from the All its source, might be regarded as an evil interlude; and this is pretty much the sense Schopenhauer has of the matter.) Piety would be this creature's virtue, tending always toward annihilation, though individual survival might be his imperious and vulgar necessity.

The specific virtue of the emerged and individual creature, for Dewey, is aesthetic experience:

"Nature," says Goethe, "has neither kernel nor shell." Only in aesthetic experience is this statement completely true. Of art as experience it is also true that nature has neither subjective nor objective being; is neither individual nor universal, sensuous nor rational. The significance of art as experience is, therefore, incomparable for the adventure of philosophic thought.

But we have been thoroughly conditioned in our pragmatic climate to think that many of the adventures of old-line or "metaphysical" thought were out of bounds, or unreal: they would set up universals without bothering to furnish one demonstrable instance. We do not wish the adventure of aesthetic thought to be so rarefied and ineffectual. The work of art as Dewey describes it above becomes too fluid for human identification.

At many places Dewey tries to conceive the role of nature in aesthetic experience in terms of perfect reciprocity with that of the human spirit. He likes to emphasize the state of harmony or equilibrium between man and nature, and implies that man brings no more than nature does to the beatific moment, and that disequilibrium is as painful for nature as it is for man. He is only a little more factual when he emphasizes the "undergoing" which man must consent to at the hands of nature if he aspires to aesthetic experience. And he remarks that the providence of nature is not strange since nature is our mother, though he adds a little sourly that sometimes she acts like a stepmother.

Yet all these metaphysical considerations are merely overtones to the solid if crowded and eclectic book which is *Art As Experience*. The great body of this work is unspeculative, and it is in this aspect that he supplies his followers with aesthetic doctrine. But I will use the plural: with aesthetic doctrines. For they scarcely consist with each other.

Much the most substantial of the doctrines is that which is always pointing out the organic or functional unity of the art-work. But the doctrine is Hegelian, or at any rate it is the pragmatic part of Hegel without the metaphysics. It is a staple of art criticism; it is in Aristotle's demonstration of the dramatic unities, and it is in Poe's critique of the short story and the poem. Undeniably, a work of art is an organism, with parts which attach functionally to each other, and produce a whole. But if it were no more than that it would be indistinguishable from a machine or scientific operation.

I should like to examine briefly three orders of knowledge which Dewey cites, and of which No. III, the climax, is art. For the distinction between I and II, I am grateful, as many others must be for whom it might have remained obscure. The distinction between II and III, for me, is not achieved.

No. I is the old-line process establishing cause and effect, in the crude or primitive sense however, as Hume and even Mill discussed it. By the old tradition of Western culture we have thought of the discovered cause which led to the desired effect as some prior natural event stumbled upon luckily and found by repeated experience to work. But the actual way of working by which this cause produces its effect eludes us; it is to be regarded as one of the mysteries of nature, whose processes we cannot fathom. Here there is indeed a great gulf or "rupture" between natural process and the human understanding. It marks science, if it be science, at its blind stage when it is a kind of alchemy.

Science advances, however, to stage No. II, and the concept of cause-and-effect is replaced by the concept of instrument-and-end. Science today is thoroughly instrumental, or at least as instrumental as it can be. For it takes the given event and studies its history backward, and continuously. Scientific research is doubtless largely a technique for bringing and holding the historical continuum of a given event under close observation. A critical connection is established, and the event which is set up as instrument bears a relation to the end-event which is transparently intelligible. The mystery disappears, and the bifurcation between natural and rational process. It is as if the instrument-member so yearned to pass into the end-stage, that it fairly jumped into its appointed place, and all but testified vocally of its purpose. (This is the tone of Dewey's treatment.)

I will make bold to illustrate the difference between I and II by an easy and homely instance. Suppose mathematical understanding is not very advanced in a certain young woman, who needs, however, to find the product of 3,478 by 7. (In this case she is inquiring into the effect of a cause, not vice versa, but it makes no difference.) She possesses some rules of alchemy, so to speak, a magical rather than truly teleological formula, which she applies blindly without understanding. The operation appears upon her paper like this:

$$
\begin{array}{r}
3,478 \\
7 \\
\hline
24,346
\end{array}
$$

But if we listen to her operating aloud, we hear something like the following, while she puts down on paper, from right to left, the numbers which I shall capitalize:

Seven times eight are fifty-SIX; carry five. Seven times seven are forty-nine, and five are fifty-FOUR; carry five. Seven times four are twenty-eight, and five are thirty-THREE; carry three. Seven times three are twenty-one, and three are TWENTY-FOUR. The number is TWO-FOUR-THREE-FOUR-SIX.

104

But if she were a true instrumentalist, she would insist on knowing what all this means. Really, the original number, the multiplicand 3,478, is itself transparently constructed, and is simply the sum of 3 thousands, 4 hundreds, 7 tens, and 8 units. (We might assume on her part an understanding of the decimal system of notation to this effect.) The process of multiplying it by 7 amounts to multiplying these parts separately but in reverse order and adding the results. The separate multiplications involve only the multiplication table; and perhaps we may believe that as a little girl she worked that out empirically, that is by addition, and did not swallow it whole when she memorized it. And now the total operation might be recorded in a more "expressive" manner, with functions made visible which she ought to have discerned anyway, something like this:

$$
\begin{array}{rl}
3,478 & \\
7 & \\
\hline
56 & (= 7 \times 8 \text{ units}) \\
490 & (= 7 \times 7 \text{ tens}) \\
\hline
546 & (\text{sum of last two items}) \\
2,800 & (= 7 \times 4 \text{ hundreds}) \\
\hline
3,346 & (\text{sum of the last two items}) \\
21,000 & (= 7 \times 3 \text{ thousands}) \\
\hline
24,346 & (\text{final sum}).
\end{array}
$$

Now this is an elementary affair for the professional mathematician, with his insight into numerical instrumentalities. Yet it has a good deal of complexity, and many niceties of functional organization—more than I have mentioned. There is not a member term which does not have a unique place and a unique role; and they all work together in perfect economy, without a gap or an overlap, to form their desired whole. This II does very well indeed, and reflects only credit on instrumental science. But when we come to No. III, the process which composes a poem or a painting, I am obliged to think that Dewey *cannot distinguish it effectively from No. II.* There was an almost extravagant respect for nature in his prefatory talk, and it is in his obiter dicta throughout, but when it comes to the terms of his actual analysis there is only the revelation of nature which squares with rational human action. The term "expressive" means for Dewey the revelation which is transparently purposive; in this usage the formulations of instrumental science would be always and necessarily expressive. The view of nature is that which 18th-century deists held, and modern science from the time of its early successes. Historically it is an important view, and valid within its limits, only it is not comprehensive of nature. And if it is true that aesthetics has been performed as soon as the art-work is demonstrated as a functional organism, aesthetics is strictly a critique of science. Naturalist aestheticians are so fond of the organization of the art work that often they exclaim that it is *perfect,* which is to strip the work of any further aesthetic possibilities. To be perfect in this sense means: to have no content which the whole construct does not require and use, and to lack none that it does; precisely like the mathematical operation above. As to the teleological or "expressive" aspect of nature, that is what the Elizabethans might have called a conceit of the natural philosophers. Nature indeed humors them, that is to say, grants them the illusion that she is eager to actualize the beneficent operation, since in it she yields terms which they find "expressive," and her whole concern is to put herself at their service. I go further: it must be conceded that the aspect of human purposiveness is fundamental to the sense of art, as it is to the sense of religion. Probably the art-work must first of all be a functional organism, and even one that is conspicuously familiar and routine, for it is to look firm and sure. But the artistic vision (like that of sound religion, if I am not mistaken) sees that nature in consenting to be humanly useful does not cease to be herself, and makes the vast depths of her natural contingency visible at the same time. In the light of this contingency her beneficence looks miraculous.

Briefly, the functional organism of the work of art carries natural context, and so the work removes itself forever from the category of science. Art is a revised version of science, restoring context. It is true that Professor Pepper accompanies his title *Aesthetic Quality* with the subtitle *A Contextualistic Theory of Beauty*; but I do not find that he theorizes boldly when he says context. I do not wish to repeat myself tediously, but will risk reiteration of an informal definition. Beauty is the impression we take of the occasion when nature assembles her materials in characteristic luxuriance, not to destroy the human design but to exhibit it well achieved, and at the same time to invest it with natural and contingent brilliance. The investing properties are not functional. The business of aesthetics is to point them out and do what it can with them in theory, while the business of scientific theory is to concern itself with the functional properties. I will offer a phrase which seems to refer too exclusively to painting but should have some adaptation to the other arts: a *functional* line characterizes the process of science, but when it is combined with a *natural line* we have the work of art.

And I remark: How different must an aesthetic naturalism be from the scientific or pragmatic article, though the latter has come to bear the title of the "philosophy of naturalism," unqualified.

4

Many naturalists are gifted with sense of reality too stubborn to be warped permanently by a dogma; especially those who are called to the aesthetic speculations. They cannot rest in the illusion that the work of art is simply, like the work of science, an organism. So they propose an alternative theory of art as if dissatisfied with the accommodations furnished it under the theory of functional organism. It is the "quality" theory, and gives off a doctrine about the "fusion" of the many qualities of the work, and one about the "funding" of the qualities. Quality, fusion, and funding are all in Dewey, whose aesthetic foundations are liberal if not conspicuously in good order. But the handsomest locus of the discussion is Professor Pepper's brilliant and increasingly famous little book, *Aesthetic Quality*.

Instead of extended or quantitative parts which function together logically in the organic whole, Pepper tries to see the work of art in quite another way: as a multitude of distinct perceptible qualities somehow "fusing" together to create still another distinct quality which is the quality of the whole. The mechanistic concept of fusion is too narrow for this context. I am struck by the fact that the latter and larger part of the book deals with the "organization" of the art-work, and discusses such topics as "scheme" and "scale," "type," "pattern," "design." And this part of Pepper's writing is good aesthetics; in fact it seems to me to shed more light per page on the science of the formal analysis, especially in painting and music, than most writings of our time. The book is one to learn from and give thanks for. But it has a curious feature. Discussion of the mode of creation of some art is apt to carry a mnemonic tag to this effect: "Of course the specific qualities of these parts must fuse successfully into a single felt whole." Why is the addition needed? It seems to nullify the careful analysis.

I presume that what really happens for the knowing aesthetician like Pepper is the revelation that an art-work never consents to be squeezed into an "organization." Yet it is skeletally put together, as it must be. Therefore an "organic" analysis is indicated for describing it. There is no other analysis which discloses such counters for the aesthetic discussion as plot, argument, design, form, structure, harmony, composition, the sequence of pragmatic human interest, the logical organization of whatever sort. In these resides no more and no less than the core of prose which assembles the poem, or the core of science which assembles the work of art. And then what we still need in the way of theory is some supplement of doctrine, like an aesthetic rider, to go along with organicism and account for the great residue of content which escapes the net of organic analysis. This residue would be the difference between, for example, the actual poem and its mere paraphrase; or between the complete painting, which represents with some fidelity the configution of its natural objects, and the ideal or geometrical configuration of its abstract design, which the represented objects play over and never conform to. A theory of residue would require us apparently to acknowledge, and dwell upon with love, the dense natural context of an imperious human action; or, if this version is easier, to stop and love the familiar individual objects of nature even at the moment when we are doing business with them. But the theory of fusion does not refer to any effect of this sort, nor does it supplement the shortcomings of the organicist theory. It is complete in itself, and it is entirely alternative to organicism.

But it would be too soon to say sententiously at this point: "So much for fusion." Some essential human impulse must be behind it. Now the qualitists under consideration are naturalists, though of superior sensibility, and they can hardly help coveting a very great *unity* for the work of art; it is with them a hazard of profession; and fusion is a form of unity. By virtue of their training in the school they are conditioned to the methodology of science, which aspires always to the completest unification of its materials under the dominant purpose of the occasion. Unification is empire, in politics, in business and affairs. To unify an area of nature, if only in theory, is to grasp it firmly with one act of perfect understanding; and natural science acquires that grasp where it can, and sometimes it vaunteth itself, whereas the habit of art is discreetly, though willfully, to disperse the view, and to intimate that nature is too various to be unified, at least against her will. I think it more becoming to attribute faulty motive to the qualitists than to construe them as monsters of no motive. Briefly, then, I suppose that when the glory of the organic analysis fails them, as they have the discernment to see it fails them in art, they improvise a kind of unification which is not organic and logical at all but fabulous, or at best "intuitive"; it is called "fusion" and, for all that can be said to the contrary, it is just as tight in operation as organism.

It would probably be the idea of all of us, and not merely that of the qualitists, that the work of art is a formidable entity, and rather more subtle than a Christmas tree. But I will risk some absurdity, to suggest that it might be wholesome for us to see it as something like a Christmas tree. For, on Christmas morning when the switch is turned on, and the Christmas tree bursts upon our prepared vision in its beauty, we have the almost instantaneous sense of an intelligible object, and we feel such assured satisfaction and completion as may amount to the "ecstasy" or the "seizure" which qualitists, from Dewey on, desiderate for their arts. But I think the experience is not too spectacular when examined. There is the strong and steady tree, beneath the lights and ornaments and gifts which are so thickly strung upon it. (For fear of spoiling the analogy let us not assign gross appetitive value to the gifts; let them be chiefly "surprises," remembrances, symbols of the general powers of beneficence which in the holy days of Christmas if not every day we would commemorate.) The tree stands up; we are confident that the accessories will not break it down. And at once we sense enough of the frequency and the quality of the accessories to know that the total object is of great magnitude in the dimension of its density, and will repay the adventure of exploring its detail. Of course the Christmas tree is an awkward mechanical affair, for it is we the bourgeois fathers, and neither infinite nature nor her artist, who have stood it up and decked it with little treasures; though these may appear contingent enough to the well-mannered explorer they are still not quite "natural" as they might appear in works of the true art faithful to nature's subtle line. But however that may be, it is certain that we are not going to exclaim about some incredible degree of unity in the composition of the Christmas tree; it would not suit the occasion. For here is the moral. It is only the sturdy frame of a small cedar which holds everything together to make an object that is technically and sufficiently one, and, looking for the "unifying principle," we say comfortably that this framework will do. But its analogue in art is just that core of common working organism which holds up any train of human attention. It is enough.

Unity is the methodological interest which the qualitists must profess in the aesthetic object, and they would like to be more exacting than the object allows them. But they have another interest which is founded better, that is, more objectively, though I think they express it badly. It is their original and persistent interest in the content of the work of art, differing radically as it does from that of a work of science.

What they are likely to say too roundly is that in aesthetic experience they "find quality"; leaving to us perhaps to infer that in science they find something else. But what is quality? No object is without it. Qualities are the properties of things and events, if that is not tautological language; and if it is, then they are the indices, the tags, by which pragmatic men determine what things and events have bearing on their hopes and fortunes. By science men isolate these index qualities and perform calculation with them in order eventually to take proper physical action upon things and events, which constitutes the "adaptation to environment." Science pursues its set of qualities in the given circumstance as the hound pursues its prey; it is in a cold fury about quality. But its operations are instrumental, and as fast as it secures the right quality it drops the item that manifested it, as an instrument which has served its purpose. It is not so with the work of art, where quality is dwelt upon, memorialized, perpetuated; and where also, it will be conceded, there is quality which comes to us fresher, more arresting, intenser, more brilliant and memorable. What is the quality that registers in this manner? Locke distinguished primary and secondary qualities on the basis of their comparative objectivity. But this distinction has scarcely survived, for we are not so temerarious now as to care to discount the secondary qualities. Much more pertinent, it might be, would be a distinction between index qualities, or functional qualities, very probably measurable and quantitative so that some science by manipulating them may proceed, and innocent or nonfunctional qualities which are merely aesthetic, do not advance any procedure, and therefore are rejected by science as professionally as they are cherished by the arts. The very same member object in the work may present both kinds of quality. For every object is a manifold of qualities, but the scientific work confines its attention to the functional qualities of its objects, while the work of art attends also to their nonfunctional qualities.

It is common for qualitists to talk a little wildly, confusing the two orders of quality, and referring aesthetic effects to the one or the other indifferently, or even rather to mere quality-in-general. But I will quote an acute passage by Professor Eliseo Vivas, now of the University of Chicago, from "The Aesthetic Transaction," his essay in the volume of naturalist essays. He is discussing the requirement of "freshness" in the aesthetic object, or "liveliness," or, to give the name which seems closest to a technical usage, vividness. How does an object transcend its routine presentation and offer itself to us as vivid or aesthetic?

> How do objects call forth fresh perception? An explanation of how this is possible would involve us in a thorough discussion of the psychology of perception. Here all we need to do is to try to state the most general principle, which is this: objects which are mere rubber-stamp duplicates of stock objects of usual experience are not likely to elicit fresh attention from man. . . . To call forth fresh perception, certain innovations and variations are required—variations which may need to be subtle or gross, depending upon the degree of encrusted habits of response they must plow up. Fresh aesthetic perception therefore operates between two extremes: the utterly familiar and the utterly new. The familiar defeats the activity, because it stimulates a patterned response, which, tending toward the automatic, hardly rises to the status of the conscious. And the new defeats aesthetic attention because it forces on us a scientific inquiry. Its newness makes it a puzzle which invites resolution; we must classify it, discover its function, get acquainted with its structure, and this is the very opposite of intransitive contemplation. . . . Whatever tends to push a thing out of the utterly familiar prototype to which it belongs, yet does not tend to make it utterly unique, tends thereby to lift it into the status of aesthetic object.

113

And suppose we should use the substance of this argument to point up the difference between a formal artistic composition and a work of technical science. I hope Vivas would not be altogether repelled by the following improvisation of my own:

> An object under scientific treatment may not exhibit more than the set of qualities functional to the given purpose. It becomes vivid and aesthetic only when it is made to exhibit from its actual manifold of qualities some that are nonfunctional also. The discourse in which this occurs freely with the objects is artistic rather than scientific. But the functional qualities are not canceled, and the operation continues to be performed even with objects now vivid, novel, and insubordinate. An operation that persists under these difficulties is evidently a perfunctory or merely formal one. The real purpose of the discourse is to recover to the objects their natural rather than their humanly useful condition.

These are flat generalizations, but they might give a direction to some aesthetic discussion. The analyses of Professor Pepper, for example, are prodigiously facile and keen, but when he is going freely they have no particular orientation; especially on the pragmatic or motivational side. They do not indicate the human attitude, or sense of values, or passion, behind the peculiar and infinitely labored actions of the artists. It amazes me to discover that such a report can be made upon any naturalist.

I return to Vivas to quote another text, which I abridge very slightly without substantive change:

> It seems to me that it is proper to use the term "aesthetic" so long as our attention concentrates on the object and does not go outside it. But this use of the term does not free us from the need to explain how we can behold objects intransitively which nevertheless embody all sorts of meanings and all sorts of values from all sorts of ranges of human experience with-

out restriction. I take this to be the central problem of aesthetics and one which must be squarely faced, particularly by a writer who is convinced that if there is one thing which the aesthetic object positively does not do, when it fully lives up to its function as aesthetic, is to point beyond itself referentially or serve as a mnemonic device.

This language relates to the strange failure of our normal interest in the scientific consequence of a work when it is a work of art. How is it possible, and what other interest can naturalists establish to take its place? I am sure that "love of nature" is not an interest which they are prone to acknowledge, with their biological views of human action. It does indeed become a leading problem, to explain an occupation with the natural objects that is to no practical purpose. Not professing to have the answer, I remark that the naturalists are our great motive-hunters, and it is right that in Vivas they have one to raise the question about this motive.

5

After "fusion," it should be easy and pleasant to present "funding." That is, at least, as I myself would construe the term.

Consider the root or concrete meanings of the two terms. Two substances are fused when they are melted and poured together, provided a chemical transformation takes place whereby a third substance is produced whose quality is unlike that of either original. It is really a case of alchemy, which is generally present in a chemical operation. The A atom and the B atom can be assigned their characteristic positions in the product molecule C, perhaps; that is stereo- or space-chemistry. The novel quality manifested by C is inexplicable; it is one of the happy contingencies of nature, whose fertility evades any managing sense that is within our power. But it is extremely hard and public fact, and I could not find the like factuality in the supposed fusion of the successive qualities of a work of art into the new quality of the whole.

To fund, on the other hand, describes an altogether more homely sort of action; to put items of property into a general aggregate or estate. If fusing is a chemical term, funding is only additive. It is scarcely that, for the items need not be coördinate, and subject to arithmetical composition. In our affairs we do not even have to reduce to monetary value the physical properties we fund, and if we die intestate they may have to be disposed of piecemeal to the heirs because unsuitable for sale at public auction. If now the properties are worth keeping, they obviously are unapt to have a common denominator and to add up to a homogeneous sum, just as they cannot be fused in some marvelous manner. And it is of immense importance to give this testimony about the knowledge funded in the course of realizing an artistic composition.

This last is not an aimless procedure, thanks to the central logic of its organism; and neither is that of a systematic tourist with a good sense of direction who goes on a well-planned itinerary to see some politico-geographical area, like Brittany. He visits no sub-area, such as St. Malo, without placing it, in scale, upon his map. Nor does he visit a place like St. Malo without having many interesting experiences, some of which attach to still smaller areas, such as a quay, or a café, or church. When he has completed his month's tour, and reviewed his notes and maps, he has funded a great aggregate of impressions, with a spatial and temporal reference for every one of them, and he may say that every one is an impression of Brittany. But what he met on the quay is not exactly a quality of Brittany but a quality of the quay of a town in Brittany. This tourist's Brittany bears an analogy with a hearer's symphony or a reader's poem such as to disarm the camp of the unificationists; though the latter items exceed the former in subtlety of relations as they exceed the Christmas tree.

Funding assigns to art a loose and comfortable sort of epistemology. It emphasizes the sheer multiplicity and incommensurability of the meanings or qualities that can group themselves under one consecutive experience. It does less than justice to the extent of the interconnections among the meanings in the work, but on the other hand it guards us against a bad and academic error, if we should look for an overnicety or meticulous formalism in these relations. I was grateful to the naturalists for making me acquainted with the aesthetic possibilities of the term.

The sequel with which I conclude, however, is ignominious. Dewey and Pepper in their use of the term have not failed to turn it masterfully to their own service, as organicists and fusionists. For some time I had made the mortifying error of having them construe the term as I did. But Pepper writes:

> We are thus able to talk about the character or quality of the Japanese print, meaning not any one perception of it, but the cumulative continuity or train of perceptions of it. For earlier perceptions have effect upon later ones, and the event quality of each successive perception becomes gradually enriched. This is called *funding*. The later more richly funded event qualities are recognized as presenting ever more and more truly the full individual quality or character of the print.

It is true that the earlier perceptions can have no relation to the later perceptions which we have not yet experienced, whereas the later, as fast as we get them, will show relations to the earlier. We have therefore a progressive enrichment of the events as we proceed. It is true also that we enrich the treasury of events by plain augmentation, or funding unqualified, and as I had conceived it; for it cannot be contended that the later events cancel the earlier events. But here we are back at the question about the meaning of any object or event; whether it has only functional meaning and is serviceable, or has nonfunctional meaning too and is itself an energetic and aesthetic object.

In any case the actual use that Dewey and Pepper make of the term is in the argument for logical organism, not fusion. It slightly impairs a reader's confidence to find that they have allowed themselves at times to offer "funding" as a synonym for "fusion." For both have slipped into locutions such as "funded or fused." Perhaps they forgot to render the school distinction between *fundo-fundare-fundatum* and *fundo-fundere-fusum*.

Beating the Naturalists
with the Stick of Drama (1945)

MR. BETHELL PURSUED LITERARY AND THEOLOGICAL STUDIES
at Cambridge, and soon after, in 1935, was contributing to Mr.
Eliot's *Criterion*—a scholar not too academic to write vigor-
ously.

In this defense of Shakespeare against modern drama[1] the
vigor is more conspicuous than the dialectical scruple. He sets
up his stock opposition in the first chapter, "Conventionalism
and Naturalism," and begins as follows:

> From time to time and from place to place the drama varies
> its position on a scale between the two extremes of absolute
> conventionalism and absolute naturalism. At either extreme
> it would cease to be properly dramatic. Absolute conventional-

[1] S. L. Bethell, *Shakespeare and the Popular Dramatic Tradition*
(Durham, N.C.: Duke University Press, 1944).

ism would work in symbols bearing no necessary relation to the things symbolized, and absolute naturalism would reproduce a "slice of life" with more than photographic fidelity. The former would be devoid of emotive power, like the symbols in algebra, whilst the latter would lack both intellectual and emotional organization.

But what is this "conventionalism"? In a common sense of the term it might be said that at the present time a dramatist is conventional if his work is naturalistic. But Mr. Bethell has the right to his own use of the term, and it should be familiar at least to Shakespearian and dramatic scholars. The studies of Schücking, Stoll, and others have made it clear that on many an occasion Shakespeare takes advantage of some convention regarded in the following sense: as a license permitting the interruption of drama by a nondramatic mode of discourse.

For the Elizabethan stage was still primitive, and primitive theater may be characterized as not yet knowing how to accomplish the whole job of drama, that is, to put the thing under the eyes and ears of the audience without departing from the rule of "imitation" or "representation." So it probably did not bother Shakespeare for an instant, and perhaps as Mr. Bethell claims it did not really disadvantage him, that in order to indicate his scene he had to hang out a sign reading The Queen's Closet, or The Forest, instead of changing the sets; there were no sets. (The modern theater with all its realism still makes expository use of the programs lying in the laps of the audience.) It is well known that Shakespeare's female roles had to be assigned to boy actors. And in illustration of the superior sense of Shakespeare's theater gained by the recent scholars: Shakespeare often failed, very likely because he had not seriously tried, to accomplish the required exposition within the drama proper, and had to use some character for extradramatic purposes; letting him

120

soliloquize, or make "asides" which the audience would hear (though it had to be assumed that the characters standing by would suddenly become deaf) or even address the audience directly; in order to explain the situation, or perhaps to set forth his own part in the play as a hero dedicated to virtue, or a villain sworn to crime. The invasion of drama by expository or narrative modes is such a commonplace in Shakespeare that characters are always reminding the audience that they are only actors in a play, and sometimes they do it so poetically that we may say they make a virtue even out of what was practically a necessity of theater. Nor should we be too dainty to accept these practices when we read or see Shakespeare; though I am afraid it cannot be guaranteed that in doing so we shall acquire something which Mr. Bethell thinks very fine, namely, the "omniconsciousness" which he imputes to Elizabethan spectators, able to break through an illusion and shift quickly from one "plane of reality" to another, and rising to metaphysical and religious powers not given to those who attend upon mere naturalistic drama.

So this is "conventionalism," and with it we return to Mr. Bethell's opening passage. Surely the "absolute" extremes of conventionalism and naturalism do not have equal status for reality. The first of this pair is scarcely a pole by which anybody, whether dramatist or critic, would think of orienting a drama, though its vis-à-vis does not seem entirely unsuited to this purpose. Absolute conventionalism would obtain if nondramatic discourse were submitted *everywhere,* till all the drama had been eliminated, and only algebra remained, or moral philosophy. But even on its most primitive level drama proposes to be dramatic, and is substantially dramatic, and the normal direction of its development is toward the completely dramatic. On the other hand it is scarcely true that a "slice of life," revealed dramatically through behavior and dialogue, must lack

121

all organization; or that ordinary drama does not have the means to reproduce it with more than photographic fidelity. It would have been plainer and safer though less exciting if Mr. Bethell had said only that drama varies its position between the dramatically impure and the pure or nearly pure.

Coming to the characteristic detail of Mr. Bethell's book, I will offer another sampling, a passage about historical drama. Shakespeare wrote "Histories," and so do modern dramatists. But with a difference:

> The modern procedure in writing historical plays for the "serious" theatre weights the playwright with intolerable chains. Not only must he secure the greatest accuracy in matters of fact, but he must endeavor to be faithful to period in portraying the minds of his characters; he must not allow them to think in terms of a later period, or even to use metaphor derived from a mode of life which would actually be unknown to them. This means that a writer of historical plays must shut out from his mind a good seventy-five per cent of his experience—the most detailed and original part of it, which he has gained in commerce with contemporary life. His writing becomes bookish and thin, and he tends to affect a style of imitation antiquity. His play, when produced, probably achieves the illusion of actuality for something abstract and remote, which has only the most general connection with contemporary life. Shakespeare, on the other hand, is able to use all the richness of his contemporary experience in writing of the past. For it is not only in "anachronisms" and occasional references that contemporary life enters into an Elizabethan historical play; in the style there is no attempt at all to preserve historical perspective, and the imagery, often clearly contemporary and "out of period," assures continuity of sharp contrast between the historical material and the contemporary experience with which it is brought into active relationship. The co-presence of such contrasting elements renders doubly impossible any mere

122

illusion of actuality; once again, the audience must necessarily remain critically alert, whilst at the same time the historical element distances and objectifies what is contemporary, and the contemporary element gives current significance to an historical situation.

He goes on to treat earnestly some patriotic and contemporary allusions in the Histories. But already in the course of this reading the close reader must have sensed in himself some passive resistances. For example, to the percentages cited. It scarcely appears that a modern must waive all but twenty-five per cent of his experience in order to write historical drama, if the subject is going to be of standard human importance; but, if the figure is correct, then it is equally hard to believe that one hundred per cent of Shakespeare's experience could express itself in the same project however liberally Shakespeare conceived it. Then the judicious reader may be mildly shocked by the charges brought against the modern dramatist's style. That it only *tends* to do something stylistically bad is a charity to be grateful for; but it would seem that this dramatist might either *employ a style of imitation antiquity,* or else *affect a style of antiquity,* and would be out of his head to *affect a style of imitation antiquity.* More important is the feeling that Mr. Bethell exaggerates the thin-ness of the antique style. If the dramatist can master it the effect is likely to be rich rather than thin, for the reason that the materials, the sounds of the words as well as their meanings, will have the strangeness of "history" for the modern audience and may secure a special attention.

But it is the concluding part of this passage, the ambitious part, that excites the worst suspicions. The "continuity of sharp contrast" seems psychologically unreal, and so do the academic involutions of the counters in the big last sentence. I think the argument whittles down principally to this, that Mr. Bethell fan-

123

cies a historical drama which bears transparent analogy to what we may call its "hot" local issues. Now it is not so fatal to naturalism if the personages of the historical drama make sententious commentary upon the significance of their own actions, for we have heard of that in life, though perhaps not very often in Plutarch. But to be made to speak specifically to the crises of the historian's own later age is another thing. Shakespeare doubtless played to some heady audiences in his capital city, but I think Mr. Bethell makes too much of his occasional contemporary allusions, and libels him. The historical drama that aims at a "current significance" is a topical drama. And this is what ought to be said about that: a topical drama is a naturalistic drama *philosophically* or *substantively* though it may not be *technically.* Mr. Bethell is falling into the naturalistic pit against which he has written a book to warn us; provided the substantive effect is the true pit, for Mr. Bethell as for us, rather than the manner of the presentation.

Elsewhere in this issue, Mr. Viertel presents an able critique of the living dramatist Bertolt Brecht. It seems to me that Mr. Bethell's argument has a curious affinity with it; curious, because Mr. Bethell might on behalf of Shakespeare feel inclined to repel the connection. Mr. Viertel thinks the mission of drama now is to be a social and political instrument, that is, a secular one, persuading to practical thought, and to worthy action; and considers Shakespeare as the protagonist of a drama that is passing, and good riddance, for its mission was only contemplative, and its auditors were supposed to go out from it feeling purged and comfortable. Yet under his exposition Brecht's technique is far from naturalistic, indeed further from it than Shakespeare's was. So here is the Shakespeare of Mr. Bethell's version of the Histories, and here is the modern Brecht, and the account is the same: naturalistic as to the philosophical effect, and nonnaturalistic as to the dramatic form.

And we know that the recipe might be exactly reversed, and still yield a valid drama. It has done so many times. How otherwise could we formulate *Agamemnon*? Here is the work of a playwright who is certainly primitive, in the plain sense of standing at the dawn of European drama. He is nonnaturalistic in his philosophy of life, which is to say that he is religious, profoundly, and also circumstantially in the manner of an orthodox Greek; he is what Mr. Bethell would call a supernaturalist. Yet he has a prococious flair for the dramatic technique which is called naturalism, and masters it to an advanced degree. It is true that Aeschylus writes in verse, and to that extent is nonnaturalist and old-school. So is T. S. Eliot of *Family Reunion,* though otherwise this modern adapts his religious theme scrupulously to a naturalistic stage development. But there are many modern plays even in prose which intend quite contrariwise to philosophic naturalism, yet fancy the sheer craftsmanship of the naturalistic theater. There is Ibsen. Mr. Bethell makes fifteen or so references to Ibsen, judging from the index, and seems to cite him regularly as the bad boy of naturalism, both ways, and not merely on the stage. But Ibsen is the author of *Little Eyolf,* of *Lady from the Sea,* of *Master Builder,* of *Wild Duck,* and such plays.

One might conjecture that Mr. Bethell's great emotional bias is against philosophical naturalism, but that while he was about it, and forgetting his semantical discretion, he decided to hit everything that goes under the name of naturalism, including a species of drama.

Mr. Bethell's antinaturalism is of the common or garden variety; super-naturalism. Since the modern mind is painfully what it is, and its commentator might well be expected in literary circles to remember the pain, and the honest travail, Mr. Bethell's antinaturalism is not perfect in dignity as it comes to us in staccato fashion, looking uncritical, irreconcilable, and of a temper most un-Shakespearian. In *Lear* he finds Shakespeare systematically presenting "nature" in its odious aspect, and asks,

> . . . may we not at least suspect Shakespeare of deliberately intending to present a world without revelation, in order to determine how far human nature could penetrate its mysteries and achieve religious and moral order apart from the gift of supernatural grace?

This defiant last phrase is as beguiling, it is as truly Romantic and evasive, as it is venerable and official. To know the truth of it would require the subtlest intelligence, the most patient study. Humility suits these considerations. And it might have occurred to Mr. Bethell that perhaps some of the bad naturalists might not be permanently excluded, first from this humility, and then from religious understanding.

Doubtless I have reported the worst of Mr. Bethell's book. It is pleasant to say in conclusion that he never wearies of pointing out the most radical of all Shakespeare's technical "conventions": it is the license he accepted to let his characters speak verse. The concession is too handsome for tough purists to grant when they come into the power; gradually it has been withdrawn from the dramatist as the naturalistic ideal has become more narrowly defined and more firmly fixed upon the public mind. And here what is nonnaturalistic as formal drama is also in sharp exception to the standards of at least the technical or sectarian branch of philosophical naturalists. There is no way of holding a dramatist accountable for the purity of his "argument" or "business" when he has the freedom of verse for transacting it; none if he is Shakespeare, or another true poet. The wealth of his allusiveness confers upon the speakers in the action a new dimension of discourse. It is extradramatic, and not "operational," and it need not be supernatural. As we become conscious of the extraordinary fullness of the poetic cognition, it is possible that we will sense a property of the created world and of godhead; that would be to have religious intimations.

Mr. Bethell's cause might still be a sufficient one if he had said nothing about supernaturalism, but staked everything on a drama that spoke in verse, and an audience that could attend to the drama and hear the verse. No other drama could be infected with so much impurity, or so happy an impurity; no other audience could have so ambivalent a sensibility. There is a great chance waiting for the close psychological study of the concrete operation of this sensibility, which Mr. Bethell has not exactly furnished. It might have consequences for all our aesthetic theories, and even cast a belated illumination upon the processes of our troubled religious consciousness.

Art and the Human Economy (1945)

THIS ESSAY REFERS TO TWO PRECEDING ONES, by Mr. W. P. Southard and Mr. T. W. Adorno;[1] there is some editorial presumption on my part in collating them and commenting them together. Special disservice is done to Mr. Southard, whose essay in the first place is a literary appreciation of Robert Penn Warren's poetry, and of a quality permitting us to think the poet is lucky in having found his exegete so soon. But Mr. Southard in the course of his thesis, and Mr. Adorno immediately, embark upon the same topic, and it is one that has a great urgency for us: the unhappy human condition that has risen under the modern economy, and the question of whether religion and art can do anything about it. It is true that the writers do not have

[1] W. P. Southard, "The Religious Poetry of Robert Penn Warren," and T. W. Adorno, "Theses Upon Art and Religion Today," *The Kenyon Review,* Vol. VII, No. 4 (Autumn, 1945).

quite the same diagnosis of this condition, but it will be noticed that they make cross references to each other unknowingly.

Mr. Adorno is evidently for collectivism in politics, but not with all the potential ferocity of a partisan, i.e., fanatically. His social ideal has no room for religion yet provides a special asylum for art. But art is curiously close to religion in his very original and engaging description of it, as a concrete monad representing the universal concretion itself; that is to say, as a construction from which the experient receives cosmic or ontological vision. What else is it for? It is not attached to the practical life which falls under the overall survey of the political economy. It is free, and Mr. Adorno awards to it an *imperium in imperio*. That is a handsome concession which many collectivists have not made.

The marvelous concretions of Proust's novel are principally of human beings in relations too tangled ever to be resolved intellectually. The element of external nature—the scene or the natural object—is never excluded, for Proust has the sensibility of a poet as well as that of a modern novelist, but for our attention it is certainly not dominant. Proust does not follow the lead of Wordsworth, returning to external nature to find God, returning there also to find—by an indirection that Wordsworth scarcely succeeded in making clear—man himself. It would seem to be a bad logical error, and I do not know that Mr. Adorno commits it, to think that God was a term of discourse which referred to the mystery of nature as long as nature was mysterious, but for the moderns who have "conquered" nature can have no particular exigency. But it would be a form of the same error—and Mr. Adorno distinctly is free of this one—to think that art deals with the "magic" of external nature but that there is nothing equally magical in a human concretion, which therefore only needs to be understood and disposed of by political science. There is mystery everywhere, as we hear it said in pious quarters; and let us say that there is mystery for the intellect in every concretion, and no possibility of thinking it out of existence.

Has art then no effect upon action, and does it not modify in any way one's commitment to action? I am inclined to think that it is in more or less ironic reaction from the fury of the practical life, and might be called "pietistic" in its mildly disparaging effect upon agents. Mr. Adorno seems to think that religion was repressive upon one or another developing form of practice, but I wonder if art does not register a disaffection with all practice. If it does not oppose something in advance, it seems at any rate to record the transaction afterward in the strangest manner. It takes us back into the concretion from which action has already delivered us.

At any picnic we have the politeness to remark for the host's benefit the local concretions of nature to which he has conducted us, but it may be that we will regard our fellow picnickers as simple and understandable creatures. The history of that might go back a long way, and even to the famous division of labor of which Mr. Adorno speaks. The division of labor made action effective by limiting sharply the apparent concretions of the natural materials which the laborer manipulated. It is true that modern life must come to terms either here or there with the whole of nature, and indeed modern life confronts a denser nature than the ancients could possibly know. But the divided laborer does not entertain this vision, nor does he know nature professionally as other than the humble if stubborn set of materials assigned him. (It might be said that the productive society at large confronts the whole concretion of nature, but so far as this purpose is concerned society is principally a fiction.) Now his own labor is not sufficient to maintain his life, but has to be integrated with all the other labors which likewise are

130

divided and dependent. He is in daily or even hourly relation with the other laborers if he cares to live. But the explicitude of these relations tends to limit the depth of his acquaintance, and to induce the feeling that the laborer in the other field has merely a kind of functional existence, or is in fact principally the other "party" to a contract. It was at the stage of the loose agrarian society, where the laborer dealt individually with his local microcosm, and did not need to relate himself incessantly to the other laborers, that acquaintance was more spontaneous and went deeper. The basis of relations then might be the curious reciprocal exploration of their human concretions, on personal or aesthetic grounds. Friendship or brotherly love, in Aristotle's account, ripens between economically independent and fully rounded men. And, even now, it is not Proust the machine-tender or Proust the draper who can dwell so long on a human history without exhausting it, but Proust the free citizen, the man of means and leisure, and even the voluptuary of human relations. He knows the human heart because his own vision, his own experience, is complete. And it is because there will be in any society men strong enough to complete their experience eventually, and no society able to repress them permanently, that we say art has an eternal vitality.

But when we say there will be men strong enough for art, we are conscious that we are saying also, men weak enough, that is, men backward enough; engaged upon the progressive division of labor yet given to hideous lapses of zeal and faith; going to the length of art by way of looking back. Is not there a kind of weakness in all this Remembrance of Things Past? I wonder that we have not heard about the "failure of nerve" on the part of artists as such, and not merely of particular writers. When I was a boy we used to say that somebody had "gone back on" somebody else. We were describing a kind of renegade, who couldn't after all go through with his pledge, and the novel individuation demanded. But in art we do not go back with any such finality.

Now we come to the terms of Mr. Southard's argument. We are far gone in our habit of specialized labor, whether we work with our heads or our hands; it has become our second nature and nearly the only human nature that we can have, in a responsible public sense. We have fallen, as Mr. Southard would say, and henceforth a condition we might properly call "decadence" is our portion; guilt and repentance, guilt followed by such salvation as can be achieved. In the forms which this salvation takes, we do go back into our original innocence, but vicariously or symbolically, not really. We cannot actually go back, and if we try it the old estate becomes insupportable; a little trial will show that. It was the estate of good animals opposing nature with little benefit of rational discourse, therefore of abstraction (the splitting off of the concept from the total image) and special effectiveness. We would not like it now. So we manage as we are with the help of salvation, an excellent thing though only for a guilty species. Salvation is simple as picnics, or games, it may be; but for superior sinners it must take a higher form, such as individual works of art, or religious exercises which are institutionalized and rehearsed in ritual. All these are compensatory concretions—they return to primitive experience but only formally; by no means do they propose to abandon the forward economy.

I find myself in the fullest sympathy with Mr. Southard's argument—up to the unexpected jump he makes at the end. It seemed that we had taken our constitutional and predestined development, and our progress was irreversible; but suddenly Mr. Southard proposes to found an agrarian community within which innocence may be recovered. I can reproach him for his phantasy with a better conscience inasmuch as I have entertained it too, as one of the Southern agrarians. And it seems to be in order to offer a brief notice about that, though I will not pretend to be representing Mr. Warren, or Mr. Tate, or others of the group.

Mr. Southard taxes the Southern agrarians for not having practiced what they preached, and that is a hit in a place where they have been hit before, though rarely by critics of his philosophical caliber. But I am struck by a slight dampness of spirit in his abjuration of the world. He says the young would seem to have made sacrifices enough in these days, as if that would be almost the greatest one yet. And it would be; it is a sacrifice which I hope he would not make. For without consenting to a division of labor, and hence modern society, we should have not only no effective science, invention, and scholarship, but nothing to speak of in art, e.g., *reviews* and contributions to *reviews,* fine poems and their exegesis; and on both sides of the line he has already given achievement. The pure though always divided knowledges, and the physical gadgets and commodities, constitute our science, and are the guilty fruits; but the former are triumphs of muscular intellect, and the latter at best are clean and wholly at our service. The arts are the expiations, but they are beautiful. Together they comprise the detail of human history. They seem worth the vile welter through which homeless spirits must wade between times, with sensibilities subject to ravage as they are. On these terms the generic human economy can operate, and they are the only terms practicable now. So the Southern agrarians did not go back to the farm, with the exceptions which I think were not thoroughgoing. And presently it seemed to them that they could not invite other moderns, their business friends for example, to do what they were not doing themselves. Nor could they even try to bring it about that practicing agrarians, such as there might still be in the Old South, should be insulated from the division of labor and con-

133

fined securely in their gardens of innocence. An educator or a writer cannot abandon the presuppositions behind his whole vocation, nor imagine that they have less than a universal validity for the region, and ought to be kept out of the general circulation as beyond the common attainment. I find an irony at my expense in remarking that the judgment just now delivered by the Declaration of Potsdam against the German people is that they shall return to an agrarian economy. Once I should have thought there could have been no greater happiness for a people, but now I have no difficulty in seeing it for what it is meant to be: a heavy punishment. Technically it might be said to be an inhuman punishment, in the case where the people in the natural course of things have left the garden far behind.

But I think the agrarian nostalgia was very valuable to the participants, a mode of repentance not itself to be repented. It matured their understanding of the forward-and-backward rhythm of the human economy. And now, for example, whatever may be the politics of the agrarians, I believe it may be observed that they are defending the freedom of the arts, whose function they understand. Not so much can be said for some intemperate exponents of the economic "progress."

As a formal definition of the art-work I have nothing to offer that would compete with Mr. Adorno's adaptation of the Leibnitzian monad. But as a natural history of the event, giving a sense of its background and its participation in the total human economy, it leaves something to be desired, and in conclusion I will try to sketch this area of meaning as it might be revealed upon a public occasion. It will be a historic occasion, but I am improvising the detail, since I do not know my facts. Let us say that it is time to unveil the statue of an eminent public man, and let it be Bismarck. His program has been notably strenuous, and it has succeeded. His very physiognomy and carriage when rendered by the faithful sculptor will betoken the audacity of his conceptions, his persistence with them, and even the habit of success. The citizens do not let their rites wait upon his death, and it is to be emphasized that these are not death rites, and in no sense exult in his mortality but in the grandeur of his career at its prime. It is only 1879, but everybody now can see his greatness, and he is already in history, a firm instance of those uncompromising human spirits who travel far from their origins and make their mark.

But there is an ambiguity in the event. In the act of turning him to stone and planting him immovably in the earth, there is a question of what these people really mean to celebrate on their festal occasion. It is as if they were not honoring the efficacious Bismarck any more than they are honoring the Nature to whom they now commit him, like a truant returned to the parental bosom. In the mound and in the pedestal upon the mound that support the stone Bismarck the earth seems to rise a little way, but still with an inscrutable dignity, to welcome him; as if his willful alienation had always been conceded, had in nowise been mortal for her, and now, if he liked, was over. The golden Rhine flows past evenly, as if he did not mind having upon his bank a thing even so sternly individuated as a Bismarck. By the art of the statue Bismarck himself is invested with a beauty whose conditions he would not and could not have fulfilled in his own person. And all who are present understand these things, perhaps without knowing it. Let us say: Those who are supposed to commemorate action are commemorating reaction; they are pledged to the Enlightenment, but, even in Its name, they clutter It with natural piety.

The Iconography of the Master (1947)

WE HAD BEST CONSULT THE PAGES OF SHAKESPEARE if we care
to see what icons are like. He is no common dabbler in his
effects. And here is the "play" called *Hamlet*; and the counters
employed are "icons," that is, "images" or "likenesses" of the
actors and their deeds and speeches. The text which we will examine is *Hamlet,* Act IV, Scene v, ll. 77–96, where the royal
but uneasy Claudius is explaining the situation to Gertrude his
queen. But the "play" of the actors is not visible nor audible to
my readers; they must rely upon the words which they read,
which they understand only if they are literate. This is what they
see on the page:

> O Gertrude, Gertrude,
> When sorrows come, they come not single spies,
> But in battalions! First, her father slain;

Next, your son gone, and he most violent author
Of his own just remove: the people muddied,
Thick and unwholesome in their thoughts and whispers,
For good Polonius' death; and we have done but greenly,
In hugger-mugger to inter him: poor Ophelia
Divided from herself and her fair judgment,
Without the which we are pictures, or mere beasts:
Last, and as much containing as all these,
Her brother is in secret come from France;
Feeds on his wonder, keeps himself in clouds,
And wants not buzzers to infect his ear
With pestilent speeches of his father's death;
Wherein necessity, of matter beggar'd,
Will nothing stick our person to arraign
In ear and ear. O my dear Gertrude, this,
Like to a murdering-piece, in many places
Gives me superfluous death.

Here again the paraphrase is simple enough. Claudius remarks that troubles do not come singly. Then he lists in one long sentence his four recent troubles; a colon marks the end of each item up to the last, which has the period; but some of the items are compounded, or attended with comment, the separation of the parts being accomplished by semicolons. (In Shakespeare the colon is chiefly for indicating a stop too big for the semicolon and not big enough for the period.) Finally, he remarks that any one of the four troubles by itself is enough to ruin him.

Now there is a well-formed sentiment presiding over even this lively and unsentimental passage. *O Gertrude, Gertrude,* begins the first sentence, and *O my dear Gertrude,* begins the last one. We may not like Claudius, who is the villain in the play if there even was one, but he shares his troubles with Gertrude, and that confers a humanity upon him. Perhaps in

137

a poetic drama every character needs a core of sentiment if the dramatist expects to give him poetic speech. But outside of Claudius' affection for Gertrude in the background, the whole quality of this speech is sensibility, and not sentiment.

We notice quickly how very "figurative" is the passage. And this suggests a good form for analysis to take. We are accustomed to concede to the poet the right to depart considerably from the grammar and idiom of the prose language. Yet it is a strange concession. The great public which has been using it since the beginnings of historic literature can scarcely have known the ground for making it. It will be said that it is to enable the poet to keep his meters. But the explanation is unsophisticated. At most it may be that the difficulty of keeping meters was the cause of his linguistic irregularities when he was a tyro; later he learned to keep tolerable meters without using disordered language, but continued to use it anyhow because now he liked it for its poetic effect. (I used to write that the young poet went over his poem to smooth out the language, and the old poet went over it to roughen the language up.) However that may be, the poets do have their poetic "license." Its latitude is wide, yet it falls readily into certain types or categories of aberration. These are what we call the "figures of speech." The Greek grammarians had a keen sense for this sort of thing, far keener than ours; they identified and named more tropes, or figures, than succeeding nations have cared to keep in their literary lexicons. In the passage before us we may regard every flaw in the thought-work as a lapse from the norm of language, and every lapse from the norm of language as a figure. But instead of listing the score or so of cases as we come to them, we shall be content to remark most of them under the headings of important figures. We need not find a technical name for every figure.

I. We may even group figures together. And first those that

fall into a group of what we may call syntactical figures, or, more properly, dystactical figures; those that do not make substantival additions to the content directly, but only indirectly, by distorting the grammar of the discourse. In this sense we have mention of Hamlet as *most violent author/Of his own just remove.* Our slight difficulty in obtaining the sense of this causes us to review the previous behavior of Hamlet, and that is actually to make substantival addition if we review more than we need to use in order to be sure that we review enough. Any difficulty in a reading, any "obscurity" is to the same effect. Here we do not know whether *remove* is active or passive. But, if active, its author is so clearly Hamlet that we should not require the given emphasis; so we take it as passive, it is Hamlet's being removed to England. How is he the author of that? But here we have the *violent;* being violent, Hamlet was removed, and he brought it upon himself. The figure would be called condensation, or ellipsis. The poetic strategist would calculate—perhaps intuitively—that elliptical statement would lead not only to filling in the parts omitted but also to exploring the substantival situation in order to find the right parts; a case where parsimony is really for the sake of excess.

Ophelia is said to be *Divided from herself and her fair judgment.* A sententious imprecision of some kind. The young lady has become schizophrenic, a split personality. One of her personalities, perhaps the one who sings bawdy songs, is named Ophelia, the other is named *herself;* the status of the *her fair judgment* is uncertain. Ridiculous consequences flow if we care to play with these terms. Even so, I doubt if we want the line otherwise; a foolish, pompous line about madness. I will suppose that it would have been idiomatic for Shakespeare to say, as we should say now, that Ophelia was not herself, and had lost her mind, or judgment.

As much containing and *our person to arraign:* wrong word order. Modern poets have nearly surrendered their license to this figure. It does not lead to much recovery of substance.

In ear and ear: elliptical, nearly foolish, yet still impressive; as if the world were too crowded, and time too short, for specifications.

In many places/Gives me superfluous death. We sense some kind of incoherence here. One point may be that not all the many deaths (there are only five) are superfluous, since one must be counted in order to make the others so. Then we question whether the other four are really deaths if Claudius is already dead. But the dystax of poets is a paradise for schoolmasters if they are provided with red pencils, and not particularly dedicated to sensibility.

II. The other great group of figures is composed of those which introduce substance directly, by naming it; and illegitimately, too, in the sense that it is foreign substance, and not merely the substance recovered to the given situation. (When a given specific object, such as the-Caesar-who-was-killed, is expanded into "great Caesar" or "noble Caesar" or "Caesar-wearing-this-mantle," that is still within the context and not a departure, and might by comparison be called a legitimate substantival expansion; and we can have that without resorting to a figure.)

The sorrows *come not single spies,/But in battalions;* metaphor. They come actually in multitudes, but that is not enough; let them come in vivid multitudes, and why not in multitudes of soldiers, or battalions? They are certainly "inimical" to happiness. But given the battalions for the way they come, the way they do not come will be as single soldiers; and single soldiers would best come in, if they came in, as spies, to "spy out the land." So they *come not single spies,* a locution even more vivid than that about battalions. It contributes to battalions, however, in making us think of the attack of an unprincipled enemy who without warning is suddenly at the stage of full-blown war with us.

Greenly: metaphorical for childishly or hastily.

It is said that without judgment *we are pictures, or mere beasts.* Metaphors. Without judgments we have "percepts without concepts," if that is possible, in respect to our knowledge; i.e., we have pictures, in our thought, and nothing else; or we are pictures. And in respect to our conduct we have animal rather than moral motivations; we are as animals, or we are animals.

Ophelia's brother *Feeds on his wonder, keeps himself in clouds,/And wants not buzzers to infect his ear/With pestilent speeches of his father's death.* A series of metaphors. The *buzzers* are the scandalmongers whose whispering is like the buzzing of flies in the ear. What they do is to *infect* not his mind but his *ear* with *pestilence;* but at this point we swing back into the tenor with *pestilent speeches.*

As to the buzzers' speeches we learn that in them *necessity, of matter beggar'd,* arraigns the king's person. As I understand it: some people are bound to arraign my person even when they have no material evidence against me. *Necessity* and *matter* are metaphorical in a sense the reverse of usual; the vehicles are not more but less substantival than the given tenors—*necessity* as compared with the-people-who-needs-must, and *matter* as compared with material evidence—and therefore might be thought to be less vivid. But our impression of actual effect here must be very different. And we consider that the rule of metaphor is to replace the less vivid with the more vivid, but the rare exception will have the value of surprise, and may be even more effective than the rule. Certainly the phrase here requires imagination, participation, expansion on our part.

Like to a murdering-piece: simile. The simile says *like,* or *as,* the metaphor does not go through that formality. Metaphor therefore would seem to be the more concealed, the more effective; simile publishes its intention and may look too artificial, inviting resistance.

III. Under separate heading I bring the figure of mixed diction, one of Shakespeare's finest and most individual usages. I am not sure whether it belongs properly under I or II above; perhaps it would go under I. The Greeks knew the figure, but in no language is its opportunity quite so brilliant as in English. The two dictions which are mixed, or juxtaposed, are the native, primitive, or folk speech, generally constituting the larger element or context, and Latin speech, generally in the position of an elegant or foppish condensation dropped into the context. The usage originated, as I think, in the reluctance of English to domesticate its Renaissance adoptions from the Latin, which would have been to lose their foreign and aristocratic tone; Shakespeare's own practice was important if not determining in the resistance.

One of the most arresting places in the entire passage, for the sensitive reader, has this kind of mixed diction for its chief distinction: *we have done but greenly,/In hugger-mugger to inter him.* The *greenly* and the *hugger-mugger* strike us as highly vernacular and countrified speech, but they lead us straight to the prim Latinity of *inter.* The common English word would have been *bury;* in the graveyard scene of this play that word occurs seven times, by my count, while *inter* does not occur once. We may say that for the *greenly* and *hugger-mugger* sort of taste *inter* is absurd, but no more than *greenly* and *hugger-mugger* are absurd for the *inter* taste. Absurdity of the kind which results in laughter, if we are prepared for it by the context; and even here, where we are following a good thought sequence, we sense something nearly comic. Shakespeare is very daring with his Latin locutions in this style. But we can go even further in our analysis. The *hugger-mugger* taste is an Id sort of taste, and

142

the *inter* taste is an Ego sort; by every character which we are inclined to attribute to these entities. Consequently in this form of mixed diction we have repeated for us on a very small scale, on a microcosmic scale, the fundamental conflict which divides the poem between the interests of the Ego and the interests of the Id.

As to the classification of Shakespeare's mixed diction, we have a substantival usage perhaps in the order of meter. It induces the sense of a certain character in the medium itself (the medium is language) when the medium ought to have no character of its own, and be gone as soon as it delivers its referent.

Other instances are a little less decisive: Latin *infect* and *pestilent* in their pure English context; and *superfluous* in its context.

Teleology of Substance

Even though we must have omitted some of the substantival usages of Shakespeare, and mistaken others, yet we cannot come to this point in the poetic analysis and postpone any further the teleological speculation. How are we to conceive the poet's interest in the substantival object when it would seem that the organic processes are regularly and perfectly accomplished through specific objects? It looks like a perverse interest; the logical positivists might well scorn it, with their ideal of rational perfection; and the pragmatists, and naturalists, with their concern for positive human goals. They would be wrong, as I think, on the whole; but not for reasons which have yet been shown; nor for reasons which will always be withheld from their peculiar orders of intelligence. I am horrified by the horror which is still being professed toward these new philosophies by apologists of poetry, as of religion. I think it too intransigeant of us, and I am afraid it will be quaint, to deny all recent ways of thinking. I should say that logical positivism is a rather specialized philosophy, but that is not true of naturalism. In naturalistic speculation, a man is nothing less than a biological and psychological organism. I cannot see why he should be more; provided of course the whole man can be figured organically, including the poet in man.

We have had a great deal of poetic theory in the past, but it has not been argued with that understanding. It has been based of course on some sort of poetic analysis, and this did not fail to disclose the wealth of "sensibilia" or "percepts" that found its way into the poem; it was evident even to the cursory observer in the form of the vivid coloration, the local energy, and the general "decorative" element in the discourse. Nor was effort spared to account for so strange a feature. One type of explanation said—it still says—that the sensibilia are not so irreconcilable, so ultimate, as they look. They are in the poem, but they make no great difference; the logic of the argument is so powerful that it takes care of them, absorbing them, assimilating them, without a residue; which means that the poem only looks like a poetic discourse but to the careful reader is only a prose. But this explanation seems dogmatic. It is not established by detailed demonstration.

Another explanation has been that the sensibilia are in the poem for the most obvious of reasons: for the benefit of certain "faculties" which needed to exercise themselves with them; the faculties in question being set down variously as the senses, perception, imagination, the feelings, the attitudes. In one form or another this position has been argued by such thinkers as Kant and Coleridge, Richards and Brooks. But it is scarcely eligible in these days. If there are "faculties," they have not been accepted into the organism in order to transact their own private business but in order to help with the organic business.

To logical positivists the form of the argument is "tautological." To the naturalists it is simply "unreal"; that is, not according to the psychical formations as we know them.

The teleology of the thought-work, if we care to isolate that, as the prose-value of the poem, is transparently clear; that of the substantival excrescences is hidden. Their purpose is hidden, and even the thing itself is not always conceded. But this looks like the description of a Freudian situation of somewhat low-grade intensity. And that is precisely what we may propose. Let us see what we can do if at once we take the thought-work to be the Ego's, the play upon substance to be the Id's. Our task is then, if possible, to rationalize the Id-motive; that is, to see what there might be in the situation of the organism, unknown to immediate consciousness, which would justify the peculiar interest of the Id if the Id could speak for itself.

The Id, in Freud's doctrine, is that part of the psyche which initiates behavior. It is the seat of the instincts which determine the human goods, or at any rate the directions or goals of human behavior. The instincts are compulsive upon the Id, no doubt, yet it is a truly psychic or purposive entity, having pleasure for its motivating principle and accepting the instinctive patterns because they bring their pleasures. Unfortunately for the Id, it is situated so deep in the physiological organism—this is why Freud's is called the "depth" psychology—that it is blind, and does not know how to obtain its desires from the outer world. But that is because it has set up a deputy, or agent, to manage its public affairs; this is consciousness, the Ego, which has the double duty of being a sensory organ, in contact with the outer world, and a reasoning or technological organ to work out the uses of this world for the Id's benefit.

All goes well until some erratic, persistent, and unintended behavior indicates to the observer that a compulsion is coming through from the Id which the Ego cannot control. Presumably there is a wish which the Id will not surrender, and the Ego, wiser than the Id and engaged in long-range planning, will not perform. Is the Id for all its blindness meddling in the faithful stewardship of the Ego? Or does the Id assert itself because the Ego has betrayed its dearest interests? Freud studied these disorders—they were precisely the phenomena which drove him to the first systematic concept of the unconscious psyche or Id—and as an arbiter pronounced rather in favor of the Ego and against the Id. He developed the technique called psychoanalysis, by which the childlike and inarticulate Id could be made to talk after all, and to reveal its secret wish. But upon the revelation the wish evaporated, it was too absurd even to talk about in the wiser language of the Ego, and the Id knew it; the Id had been talked out of its wish. In the course of Freud's career of speculation, however, he seemed to become more and more sympathetic with the Id in its conflicts with the Ego. The Ego with its principle of reason was too enterprising, too ambitious; it involved the whole psyche in adaptations which brought anxieties and deprivations too great to be borne. In a late work such as *Civilization and Its Discontents,* Freud is fully sensitive to the burden that rests upon the modern spirit and threatens civilization with collapse. And since his death we have had the issue of orthodoxy mooted between two schools of Freudians: the sociological one, which believes that the Ego must keep the ascendancy, and repress the Id; and the biological, which believes that this policy is too dangerous, and the Id must come nearer to having its way. It suits our present interest, as apologists of poetry, to incline decidedly towards the biological view.

Of course, I have given a reduced and simplified version of Freud's doctrine, and it may well be abhorrent to a good Freudian. For instance I have neglected to tell of Freud's frequent excursions into "metapsychology," in which he carefully

146

blueprinted the possible neural mechanisms which would support the conscious-unconscious compounds of behavior as he liked to figure them on the psychological level.

Perhaps on the strength of my representations we can at least figure something of the responsibilities we undertake if we improvise a speculation which Freud never fully and systematically made: about the apparent "sentimental attachment," or "fixation," of the psyche with respect to certain natural objects, going beyond practical interest in these objects as the source of gratifications for the Id. It would look as if we must promise to do several things. One thing we may pass over without bothering about: the attitude of the brisk managerial Ego, the practical reason, to this attachment; it is devoted to aggression against the environment, and the best it can do with the objects in question in their strange new status is to make sure that they do furnish their plain uses. But among the things we seem to undertake is, first, to identify the kind of pleasure which the fixation brings to the Id, though this may not be quite what the notoriously libidinous Id is supposed to want. Freud's own psychology is hedonistic with respect to psychical motivation, but on the other hand his hedonism must be the most comprehensive and most versatile on record. Then we ought to be able to know that there is a possible physiological mechanism enabling the supposed fixation to work; but so far as I am concerned this provision will have to be waived. The only comfort I can take is from the general understanding that the psychical mechanisms always precede the neural mechanisms in the order of our speculations, and often have to wait for them. Finally, since a speculative psychologist must also be a biologist, we must see how our psychic fixation serves the long-range needs of the biological organism. This last would be ultimate motive, or final cause proper. It seems not really to matter very much whether we regard some mechanism as instituted by a natural providence—such as we denote by Mother Nature, or just Nature, capitalized—which we can never isolate and identify; or regard it as arrived at in the course of the mutations of species and stabilized because those creatures who had it were the ones "calculated"—though there was nobody to make these calculations—to survive on the strength of it. Either way, we are accustomed to think of the "purpose" of the mechanism; and of course the term itself is teleological if we go back to the Greek, where mechanism is something contrived. But given the mechanism, we see at once its relation to the Id's pleasure; the latter provision is a sort of immediate cause, or sanction, which pulls the lever and puts the mechanism into operation.

Poets and Flatworms (1952)

THIS IS NOT THE FIRST PRINTING of the prose *Enjoyment of Poetry*,[1] nor of that work enlarged by five leading essays from the author's other books. Nor is it the first printing of the poetic *Anthology*; I believe this never appeared by itself but only, in 1939, along with the enlarged *Enjoyment*. The present volume seems, then, to be only a fresh printing of the 1939 volume with a new general introduction and slight revisions. But that is good. The publishers needed the new printing to satisfy a continuing demand. If we reflect that it is wanted by college classes as well as general readers, we will conclude that Max Eastman's theory of poetry is one of the agents in a sort of poetic enlightenment in our time; and if we will now

[1] Max Eastman, *The Enjoyment of Poetry, With Anthology for the Enjoyment of Poetry* (New York: Scribner's, 1951).

follow his theory through the whole work as will attest that he belongs in the company of our superior critics.

It is my impression that Eastman's work is really not very well known in certain critical circles, and that this is perhaps because of a fierce but minor controversy which once raged between other critics and the polemical person who was this one's alter ego. But he does not include here the old essays on "The Cult of Unintelligibility" and "Poets Thinking to Themselves"—papers which would define the period in its modern phase. Its only holdover in the present volume is in its effect upon the choice of the modern entries to the *Anthology,* where we miss almost entirely the harder poems of Hopkins, Yeats, Eliot, Tate, Auden, and Thomas, though a good many of them would seem demanded in a representative exhibition.

Max Eastman requires the reader of poetry to have some theoretical understanding of the experience, and it is my observation that the reader if he is spirited and intelligent—if for example he is a smart young collegian—intends in our time by all means to have it. (There is no use telling such a reader that he mustn't have it, that it is dangerous. He will want it all the more.)

Eastman was one of the pioneers in a certain insight into poetic language which waited till an astonishingly late time to disclose itself clearly. It came to him in a figure which he made famous. Take a crowd of people going to the city on a ferryboat, and see how they all fall into two classes: those who are inside, planning the business of the day, or else merely killing an idle time; and those who are outside, looking at what is happening on the water and enjoying what they see. The first are the *practical* kind; the second are the *poetic* kind. It is a bold dichotomy for the apologist of the poetic people to risk; they may look too suggestible, and unprovided with sound resources of their own. It is still bolder when he applies the trope to actual poems. In a poem Eastman always finds some familiar occasion which makes a practical sense, but within which the poet is stopping constantly to look at those features which have nothing to do with the practical procedures. He is right about this, of course. Analysis reveals very surely the large measure in which poetic attention is directed to the (practically) irrelevant areas of the situation; in which the activity of perception is excessive. In this there is indicated some stubborn exception to the rule of behavior; fit to challenge the psychologist and even, eventually, the biologist. The nature of art, says Eastman, is "to shun generality and cleave to the unique nature of each individual experience." We will understand from this that practical language (as in business or science) generalizes the useful (or operational) aspects of the situation and excludes the others; but that poetry spreads its interest over any or all of the other aspects and attends to the irrational wholeness of the situation, which is unique and inviolable by generalization. He enforces this analysis easily and ingeniously through a great variety of poems, and brings his reader finally into a rather close understanding of the peculiarity of language as we have it in the most approved poetries.

The analysis is not only right, it is forthright. It might be said, but I should not say, that he advertises the illogic of poetry indiscreetly. But I should not say, either, that Mr. Eastman is like Mr. Blackmur, with whom it is a rule to leave the mysteries mysterious, except where his readers have the very highest qualifications. Let it be said that discretion does not enter into the consciousness of this able but ingenuous analyst. What he means is to find the truth and then see what happens. We will question only his reaction when that happens which we must now think was bound to happen.

Many critics in our time study their poetry with this insight, and some must have got their instruction in it from Eastman. Accordingly they pore over their poetic texts to explore the "richness" or spread of the meanings, and to remark the technical ways by which the poets divert from the practical kind of discourse without seeming to be conspicuously out of order. Yet it must be added that more and more we encounter critics of the critics of poetry who declare that this particular insight is a commonplace, and they are wearied of it. If it is a commonplace we must thank the present critics of poetry for having expounded it well, for it is surely recent. But if it has grown tiresome, that must be because the critics of poetry have tended to rest in the amorphous experience which they make of the poem without finding there, or seeking, anything to bind it all together or to engage with some notable human concern in the reader. And the critics of the critics of poetry are scarcely themselves going to undertake the latter job; the likelihood is that they are principally critics of fiction, and fiction does not seem to depart from the practical line quite so scandalously as poetry does, and perhaps their interest in poetry is taken mostly insofar as poetry like fiction is able to say anything practical and direct. So in an age of unusual critical achievement we have managed to arrive rather quickly at an excruciating impasse: with cold-blooded critics of poetry working away at what sometimes appear to be the merest exercises with words; and warm-blooded critics of the critics of poetry reproaching their exercises, and perhaps about to reproach their poetry too.

How confidently, twenty years or so past, were some of us offering a new "understanding of poetry"! I will not say, how brashly; for the innovation was real, it was momentous; but it was not complete, and now it has bogged down at a most embarrassing point. In the Academy the verbal analysis has pretty well secured its place and tenure, but its end products are only half-finished, and their ragged showing does not alleviate the original apprehensions of the opposition. Now Eastman is by no means unaware that the poetic objects at this stage, after analysis has worked on them, may easily awaken repugnance in some readers who might have responded to them warmly in the first place. But do not imagine him saying that this is as yet scarcely a decisive consideration, that it would be too much to expect the whole truth about poetry to be revealed at once, and that the verbal analysis reveals truth so far as it goes. What he actually says is that poetry is to be understood precisely in the diffuse aimless-looking character which analysis attributes to it; precisely and finally. And to give some sort of standing to that character he dips into epistemology, psychology, and biology—into the speculative areas where these are really the occult sciences. It makes an interesting reading, but I do not believe it will quite do.

We can never throw off entirely, says Eastman, that logico-practical form of behavior which is primary; yet it is possible within the outline of the pattern to impede the practical response and even to inhibit it. This is what the poet does. (Eastman never attaches enough importance, for me, to an element of concealment in the poetic language, as when we speak of its tropological "devices"; I imagine it is essential that the poet *seem* to be within the norms of focused discourse so that the reader, and the poet too if that is to be the way of it, may be attending to the proprieties consciously, and to something else, something compulsive, unconsciously.) Accordingly we obtain without restriction the objective content belonging to the given situation but lost in the practical reduction of the situation. And the big content is what we enjoy. The name which Eastman likes to give to the inclusive miscellany is just "experience"; not "proper," but unqualified. We enjoy poetry because we enjoy experience. If the practical person has experience (as we can imagine him claiming that he has) it is only partial, for he does not allow himself to have the whole of it, and he is so strenuous with what he has that he would not enjoy it if he could.

Of course poetry if challenged has to bow to the priority of the practical activities. It is when there is no great practical urgency, when there is leisure, that the animal energies in us look for suitable activities to release them, and come upon— poetry, and other arts. But one does not readily find the theoretical consideration whereby the quieting of our primary wants for a time should lead us to invent a new *kind* of interim activity, and that a useless one. It may be that we cannot sleep off the interim period, or vegetate in blissful euphoria, as the lower animals appear to do. Why not spend our holiday like the busman, making pastime of the practical activity at which we excel? (We might repeat the best of our practical triumphs, in sedentary recollection or by some active drama, and take the pleasure of honest vanity; or rehearse an imaginary triumph, and take the profit of being the better prepared for it if it comes.) Or, if we must have a change (to rest certain muscles, so to speak), why not retain our even virtue by trying other activities equally practical in form, like digging a ditch, or counting the pebbles, or working in the laboratory, or studying accounting? It does not seem that an aesthetic activity—which analysis testifies is impractical in form—is indicated automatically upon the occasion of a leisure. But the converse would hold very well. We do feel that a certain leisure is indicated upon the occasion of an aesthetic activity.

"Experience" in Eastman's total and leisurely sense is thought to stand up well, to repeat itself in poem after poem, because it is provided with its specific sanction, and that is—not "pleasure," that ancient but now discredited face-saver when we cannot tell what some habitual behavior is for, but—"enjoyment"; the title word. Is it such an improvement? The idea of enjoyment feels as tepid for me as does my thought of the disorganized experience which Eastman describes. We shall be loath to believe that this term could ever register our real poetic passion, or Eastman's. And as for establishing the poetic kind of experience as a universal animal norm, that would take a lot of doing. Would it not be sufficiently flattering to the poetic theorist if he could establish his kind of experience as one peculiarly suited to the psychical economy of his own species? I am not won by the cited studies of the biologist who found that a well-fed flatworm will sometimes be activated strongly for two hours at a time, the activity consisting in showing signs of interest in some object nearby (incipient practical response) but always quickly leaving off (inhibition of practical response) to go through the same motions with the next object. The flatworm's behavior looks impractical enough, in fact it looks like a parody of the activity which Eastman finds in poetic experience. I do not understand it. But as a small-scale poetic experient myself I wish Eastman might have said flatworm with a smile.

I do not feel ambitious here to try to tell Eastman what he ought to have done about this logical disorder in the poetry, besides accepting it as the whole point of the thing. Who could tell him that with any confidence? But after the analysis of the logic of the poem, or even before it as the saving good sense which we start from, there would seem to be needed some acknowledgment of the actual warmth and feel, and the powerful psychic focus, with which poetry comes into our experience. Psychology is harder than verbal analysis. Yet it must occur to us about the aesthetic theories generally—all that we know, it may be, though we may have tried a good many—that they come to grief early because they are not prepared to discern a character of diffusion in the art-object which cannot be assimilated into the primary form of intelligence; or they fail further along, more decently, when they are aware of that much, but then cannot think of some hidden and defiant purpose which the experient might grasp with entire familiarity without knowing what he did, and which would be of a dignity and value proportionate to his enormous concern. And that is as far as I venture to go. Meanwhile, I am sure we must look long before we will find the theorist who has sailed past the first breakdown more safely than Eastman, or more jauntily.

Why Critics Don't Go Mad (1952)

IT GIVES ME A MILD ASTONISHMENT when I discover that critics of poetry do not really go mad. That seems to be the honorable prerogative of the poets, in whose train the critics follow, though not that far. But the critics have a great and public stake in poetry, and in the fate of those fluent existences, epiphanies, and "levels of meaning" which poets call into being. Especially the modern critic; who thinks he must know the ultimate reality of the poetic visions, and who may say if he likes that his precursor, the *Ur*-modern, was Coleridge, whose inquiries into the nature of poetry were frankly metaphysical, or religious. So our gifted critic will get himself quickly into the intangibles of the subject, and thence into metaphysics, that universe which it is very hard to traverse, where the treacherous skies seem always about to thin out and clear, and the jostling elements seem about to precipitate their solid substances and assume fixed places. But these are events which do not readily occur, at least without the benefit of dogma which makes them occur. To the modern critic (who is perhaps among the presentable instances of modern man) the ancient religious establishments may seem to have thought they found their solid ground too easily; it is as if religion took it for granted that it had achieved its form and station once and forever, yet still there had to come a "modern" time when everything was called into question and religion had to start all over again at the speculative level; and the second speculation is bound to be more adventurous than the first. But at any rate the critic in his own speculations is going to have many a moment asking himself if he sees what he thinks he sees, and if this is really the life for him. There is a bad sense of lostness, made the worse because he cannot take his trusting readers into his confidence. And now comes the period when he awakens in the night and tosses on his bed. It is when I think of his pains at this stage that I wonder why madness does not come to his aid. Heaven does not appear to accord so blank and absolute a relief to the critic, but only one that is humanistic and probationary. What happens is very sudden: an explosion of laughter, as the honest critic confesses that he cannot support his great ambitions, let other critics support theirs or not as may be; after which he will turn over and sleep like a babe, to awaken to birdcalls by daylight like a man restored, for the time being. The critic's happiness is not even contaminated by any need to make a public confession. But his next ensuing essays almost make up by the modesty of their range what they lack, to the surprise of his regular readers, in the old daring and subtlety.

It will be apparent that I think of the critic very certainly as a good man; a man of integrity pursuing an uncertain career. He will not go mad. And parents may be advised, if they ask advice, that they need not fear to entrust the good young men, their sons, to him at the university, if they can qualify for the courses. They will be made acquainted among other things with the soul of modern man, and that is something which is in store for them anyhow, one time or another, and more or less.

Mr. Cleanth Brooks has for some years, I think, been teaching Milton to a *corps d'élites* of pupils, and now comes his new book in exegesis of the Minor Poems.[1] This is the early Milton, but already he is a serious poet; I think we may well say he is a religious poet. And Brooks has advanced steadily in seriousness, and here will be thought of as a religious critic.

It seems to me that Brooks just now is probably the most forceful and influential critic of poetry that we have. But this does not imply that his authority is universally esteemed and accepted, for it has turned out even better than that. Where he does not gain assent, he arouses protest, and countercriticism. His tone toward other critics is that of an independent, and his tone toward scholars who are occasional critics is cool. This is why a new book by Brooks is a public service. The book on Milton will stir up some waters that may have grown brackish. There are likely to be requitals made upon Brooks by the rival critics, and the scholars, but after that there will be soul-searchings, and I shall not be surprised if it proves finally that Brooks will have touched off a Milton revival, and caused our human and poetic understanding of this poet to reach a new level of intelligence.

And of course there will be readers who will go all the way with Brooks as if under a spell. Brooks is a spellbinder. I believe the peculiar fascination of his view of poetry is due to its being so close to the ancient doctrine of divine inspiration or

[1] Cleanth Brooks and John Edward Hardy, eds., *Poems of Mr. John Milton. The 1645 Edition, with Essays in Analysis* (New York: Harcourt, Brace, 1951).

159

frenzy. For Brooks the poem exists in its metaphors. The rest of it is negligible. He goes straight to the metaphors, thinking it is they which work the miracle that is poetry; and naturally he elects for special notice the most unlikely ones. Hence paradox and irony, of which he is so fond. Now if you count little ones with big ones the two figures must be about as ubiquitous as any we have; they are easy to find once you are searching for them. It is paradox when you find something which in its bearing looks both ways, pro and con, good and bad; irony when you have something you thought was firmly established in the favorable sense, as good, and pro, but discover presently that it has gone bad for you, and is contra; the one is a pregnant ambiguity, the other is disappointment where you had least reason to expect it. The instances may be petty, and indeed the paradoxes may be only the accidents of words. There might be found somewhere fifty which Brooks has blown up into a dignity they can hardly sustain. But now and then there will be a paradox or an irony which is vivid, and crucial too, for great issues turn on it. So, and rightly, Brooks pounces. Then he proceeds to wrestle as much of the poem as possible under it as the "dominating" figure; it is likely to have philosophical or religious implications; and there is his sense of the poem. I do not seem able to describe the procedure without making it seem capricious. Brooks's method, however, is a homiletic one if I am not mistaken. In my boyhood I heard many a sermon preached where the preacher unpacked the whole burden of his thelogy from a single figurative phrase of Scripture taken out of context. Brooks heard them too. The fact is that Brooks and I were about as like as two peas from the same pod in respect to our native region, our stock (we were sons of ministers of the same faith, and equally had theology in our blood), the kind of homes we lived in, the kind of small towns; and perhaps we were most like in the unusual parallel of our formal educations. So we have more in common than we can have acquired separately. We have diverged a little. From my present point of vantage I find I am more captious than I like when I confront some of Brooks's departures, yet it is with the feeling, if he will permit, that I am contending with my alter ego.

Brooks's particular theologism resembles that of Scotus, who preached as all critics know the individuality or *haecceitas* of the well-regarded object. He does not want the poem to have a formal shape, but simply to unfold its own metaphorical energy; at least this is the impression we will take from his theoretical discussions, and many of his applied criticisms. And it will follow that you, the reader, must not recite in your own prose the action that takes place in entirely different terms in the poem. (The *quidditas* is not the *haecceitas,* the "paraphrase" is not the poem.) If you do you may be swept away into the ultimate depravity where all the readers have only a "scientific" intelligence. But what have we here? I believe that here is precisely where the modern criticism came in: in the new (or rediscovered) sense that the poetic object must be defended in its full and private being. But many critics now have thought they could assimilate this revelation and go on. If the poem has to be defended in the wholeness of its being, what of that character in the poem which makes it discourse? In whatever terms, the poem has generality and definition, if anybody wants them; it remains, if the lexicographer looks at it, a species of Aristotelian discourse. Thus it has a beginning, middle, and end, if the argument is sizable enough to bother about such things; and otherwise there is the "point" of the poem, the act of predication, or the sheer core-object, with such qualifications as may appear; and everywhere that minute kind of order which we call syntax. To so much logical formalism the metaphors and brilliances have to adapt, and surely it is very advantageous for them. They have two natures in one, and Brooks should be delighted by that

161

paradox. A poem in itself is one of the most various objects in the world; and this is besides the limitless variety between one poem and another. Twenty critics will enter the same poem and come out with twenty different reports; yet every one may be right, even the one who has found only a "moral," or a doctrine of faith. Are we going to defend this poem by locking it up against people who want their vital but vulgar "uses" of it? And should we do something about locking up nature likewise? Nor is the poem destroyed by use any more than nature is. I think I am saying all this because I have finally conceded that I must have had a little bigger bump of discretion than Brooks did; it is an ignominious deformity.

As for the learned scholars. I am worried lest the critic may not receive the whole benefit of them, or at any rate the benefit of the rare and elect spirits among them. Now criticism is literary judgment and speculation; and learning, though it is nonpareil in respect of possessing its "facts," may have very little of that character. Yet there is a possibility. Brooks will take his critical method and put it to work with a fury, and a spate of words; I in my degree have been ready with a gabble of my own. But at my shoulder I have sometimes seemed to sense a strong silent presence attending and watching me. It is not Virgil, for he attends the poets; this Guide for the critics, as I sense his presence, is the Great Scholar, so modest that he is anonymous, and in my vision I have never been able to identify him; but perfect in his attainments; possessing the sense of the art as wholly as he possesses the text, in beautiful proportion and justice, yet intuitively, without an effort; it is precisely because he has been a faithful scholar that this grace has been added unto him. He causes me to be apprehensive that my kind of criticism may be so partial as to belittle the poem, for he will know it at once, and it will be painful to see him register his embarrassment. Is he the figment of a bad conscience? I do not know if he exists in our time. But he ought to. And then comes a consideration which is a deplorable anticlimax; I think he ought also, nowadays, to have a little of our gift of gab, Brooks's and mine; else I do not see how he will make his admonishing presence felt to the young men rushing into criticism.

One of the items of the 1645 Edition is, of course, that popular pair, *L'Allegro* and *Il Penseroso*; and here Brooks's analysis is a holdover from the book of five years ago, *The Well Wrought Urn* (New York: Harcourt, Brace, 1947). For once, Brooks runs pretty well through the lengthy argument of the pieces. It is not according to his principles, before the present book at least, but he can do it under color of giving the views of the other critics. His dialectic as he goes along has a great deal of animation; and I will not forget to say that, on the whole, this essay is the best writing I have seen on the paired poems. But at last Brooks elects the decisive figure which he thinks will hold everything together. It is the figure of light-vs.-shadow, with the shadow which pervades *Il Penseroso* really brighter than the light of *L'Allegro*; and Brooks has made a strong bid. The text which supports the paradox is a passage near the beginning of *Il Penseroso* describing the goddess Melancholy:

> Whose Saintly visage is too bright
> To hit the Sense of human sight;
> And therfore to our weaker view,
> Ore laid with black staid Wisdoms hue.

Brooks explains that "the black of night, 'staid Wisdom's hue,' is merely a necessary veil to conceal a brightness in reality too intense for human sight." Then he boldly connects this passage with the passage near the very end, where the pleasures of the melancholy man grow decidedly religious, and turn on his seeing the "dimm religious light" of the church windows. The dimness of the religious light is an anti-Platonic image which seems to me entirely Miltonic. And it is much to my own taste. (I am hurt by the glare to which Plato's philosophers coming out of the human cave are subjected; or for that matter Dante's Pilgrim coming perilously close to his Heavenly Vision; even in imagination my eyes cannot take it.)

Brooks's essay is so good, and his election of the one big metaphor so striking, that I do not mean to enter any more of my pedantic objections, but only to ask for something more from him. After all, the essay which suited its original purpose has been transferred to a book which presents Milton; and in this book Brooks as a commentator has to attend to many things which would spoil a formal essay, even more an informal one. One of the favorite theses of the book is the contention that Milton is not so close to the Spenserian school stylistically as he has generally been put, but closer to the so-called "metaphysical"; which he argues at a number of places by showing that beneath the "marmoreal surface" of Milton's verse there is an energy of language which is not Spenserian at all but more like metaphysical. Now it has been said that Brooks's criticism provokes Brooks's critics to criticism; very well. The jog-trot of the two poems here, putting the Jolly Man and the Pensive Man through their paces, is very informal indeed, and we would say that it is relaxed, if we did not have the close methodical cross references continually passing from one poem to the other. The tetrameter lines do not have the logical tightness of metaphysical poetry, the couplets scarcely have the logical definition of couplets, and the composition in its parts and as a whole is not metaphysical. It jingles. The earlier poem on the Marchioness of Winchester seems at least to have been conceived metaphysically. It begins,

This rich Marble doth enterr
The honour'd Wife of *Winchester,*
A Viscounts daughter, an Earls heir,

but it quickly loses its headway, and Brooks observes acutely that Milton's failure with this and a few other poems may have helped "to estrange him from the explicitly 'conceited' and witty poetry of Donne." I am suggesting that there might be a comparison between Milton's tetrameter couplets and those of a metaphysical poet, without reference to the witty conceits. And suppose we glance at the "Horatian Ode" of Milton's friend Marvell, though that came twenty years or so later. Marvell scores a great success with his meters there, and doubles his triumph by composing his stanza out of a pair of tetrameters followed by a pair of trimeters! A *tour de force* in the short style, I quote several stanzas, which of course are not to be taken as consecutive:

> So restless Cromwell could not cease
> In the inglorious arts of peace,
> > But through adventurous war
> > Urged his active star. . . .
>
> Could by industrious valor climb
> To ruin the great work of time,
> > And cast the kingdom old
> > Into another mould. . . .
>
> That thence the royal actor borne
> The tragic scaffold might adorn;
> > While round the armed bands
> > Did clap their bloody hands.
>
> He nothing common did or mean
> Upon that memorable scene,

> But with his keener eye
> The axe's edge did try.

In these stanzas the metaphysical effect does not depend particularly upon wit, nor yet upon the well-known extended conceit employed by the school. It is an effect possible to poets who are weighty yet idiomatic; polite conversationalists, perhaps, who do not have to make speeches in order to offer their observations. This style we should have to describe as a "grave" or "pithy" style, as distinguished from the "full" or "periodic" or Spenserian style. Marvell was strong yet supple to the point that he could turn on a sixpence; or at any rate a florin. Milton did not like to have his movement cramped. He kept his swelling periods, which at many places are sure to be more compacted than Spenser's. His most idiomatic style is probably to be found in the occasional secular sonnets—some of which in our language have no superiors.

Milton did not manage his tetrameters with metaphysical skill. But in the very first of his important poems he had a fling at the couplet of trimeters, and it is most engaging. Perhaps the trimeters compelled him to break the long pentameter stride to which he was already becoming habituated, as the tetrameters did not quite because they were so near to pentameters. I quote from the "Hymn," composed at the age of twenty-one:

> And sullen *Moloch* fled,
> Hath left in shadows dred,
> His burning Idol all of blackest hue,
> In vain with Cymbals ring,
> They call the grisly king,
> In dismall dance about the furnace blue,
> The brutish gods of *Nile* as fast,
> *Isis* and *Orus,* and the Dog *Anubis* hast.

But Milton here is not risking all on the trimeter couplets. They take the stage very jauntily, and speak up very clearly, but the scene has not really been turned over to them. The long lines are always waiting to step forward and complete what they have started. It is needless to say that it is all very beautiful, and one could hardly have predicted at this moment what the new poet was going to do.

It is my impression that the metaphysical poets have a sharper metrical sense, and can do more work with it, than the other poets of English; and that the reader to whom they do not communicate this sense is missing badly. I have intimated that they do not jingle. But often they will jangle; and by premeditation, for that is one way of advertising the metrical form of the composition. Thus,

> All whom the flood did, and fire shall, o'erthrow,

which comes from the poet who cheerfully submitted to the critical opinion that he "deserved hanging." There are even more startling instances, but I choose this because it is the line of an obvious sonnet and therefore as everybody knows must rate as an iambic pentameter. The reader of poetry with a veteran's competence does not live who can come to this line for the first time and not reread it, once or three times, before he can pass on. It is one of the special incidents of the grave style.

In the Marvell stanzas which I have quoted above (I had inadvertently written "marvelous stanzas") there is neither jingle nor jangle, but there is a tightness; and what there must not be is any sense on our part of what has been prettily called a "felicity" of diction; not if the term would indicate our feeling that the meters were not very hard taskmasters anyhow, and the phrases had managed to fit in without the slightest trouble.

It is depressing when a reader tells us how very "natural" the meters seem. For it would then be as if the meters, or the poetic understanding which thought it was respecting the meters, were ceasing to function, and the meters did not know their own importance. Meters activated, as they are when the metaphysicals use them, seem at first to be restrictive, and obstructive, upon the flow of the language, but actually they are what makes the phrases shine. The Marvell lines individually, if we could now isolate them in imagination, i.e., as independent bits of language on their own, too short to be identified as anything but prose, may well have very little distinction; those of the second quoted stanza are in a rhetorical commonplace. But that is not our sense of them as they stand.

At this point I would propose to Brooks a new overall conception of the poem. A little while ago I was urging him to accept the logical form of the poem as something fixed and— for the hardheaded English-speaking public—invincible; which the showy metaphors, episodic or "dominant" as they might be, had better make their peace with, especially since it would do them no harm; and I had the idea of a poem as a great "paradox," a construct looking two ways, with logic trying to dominate the metaphors, and metaphors trying to dominate the logic, and neither, or both (as we have it in paradoxes), succeeding. But now I suggest that we must reckon with the meters too, and the poem assumes the form of a trinitarian existence. For the meters in turn enforce themselves against the logic and the metaphors, but against resistance. Since Brooks likes such terms as "equilibrium," and "organic structure," I am proposing still handsomer effects, in that family of effects, than even he has allowed for.

But by this reckoning the stock of the metaphysicals would go pretty high, and might that not be a danger to the position of Shakespeare, or the position of Milton? I believe not. If

Brooks and I were being landed on the desert island, I have no doubt that the books we would severally take along would be the same books, and chosen in about the same order, and we would read them in unison. The metaphysicals achieved a high lyric perfection; such a rounded and many-way perfection, I imagine, as a Dante essayist might attribute to Dante if Dante had been their compatriot and had lived in the early 17th century. But the metaphysicals could not write epics, nor plays. And here again we have a great and proper equilibrium, such as a humanist must like very much. Every poet finds his place in the company of poets, and there is no necessity for killing one poet to make room for another.

The Concrete Universal (1970)

IN 1954 I READ THE BOOK of Professor W. K. Wimsatt, Jr.,
entitled *The Verbal Icon* (Lexington, Ky.: University Press of
Kentucky); and I wrote an essay about it.[1] But now it appears
that I have lost the book, though I still have the essay. I am
sadly disgraced. But perhaps I am part lucky; I feel obliged to
give my essay a few rather close passages from Hegel to support
Mr. Wimsatt's discussion; even though, in 1970, it is sixteen
years after the original showing.

But I must refer to my old document to say that Mr. Wimsatt's book was a collection of essays about critical procedure,
their hazards and "fallacies," and how to make them secure. I
credited him as a scholar of reasonable temper who had read

[1] "The Concrete Universal: Observations on the Understanding of
Poetry, I," *The Kenyon Review,* Vol. XVI, No. 3 (Autumn, 1954).

nearly everything. Being at Yale, and in a superior literary environment, he must have associated with two old friends of mine, Professors Brooks and Wellek; and on the whole must be regarded as another New Critic, a late and worthy one. But as to the new portion of this essay, I must first of all congratulate him with respect to a later book, *Hateful Contraries* (Lexington, Ky.: University Press of Kentucky, 1965). It is even better in its range and decisiveness than the earlier work, and I must think of the author as one of the most knowledgeable explorers we have encountered in our time, haunting the still pools and the brawling rocky streams of verse.

Suddenly, however, I become aware that those Yale professors, all of them, are perfectly capable of withholding their favor unmercifully from faulted poets; but are not inimical to those of grace and power. I am wondering if the young poets who are gifted with a comic sense are not entitled to some amusement when they discover a peculiar fix, or bind, in which their poems are going to get their going over, and to be rated and berated accordingly; but by strangers who have not been solicited in the first place, and furthermore cannot communicate except in prose. But generally we may believe that the young poets come to like these unauthorized sharpshooters, if they feel safe enough. So the learned and capable outsiders may work beautifully to the advantage of at least the smart poets who take proper note of every suggestion; and the high-ranking poets in turn delight their monitors, first by being so good themselves, and then by contriving for their patrons' pleasure such creature moods and comforts as Aesthetic, and Religion, and Philosophy.

Mr. Wimsatt's book title is explicit. It mentions "icons," which is to say that the book supplies artificial images of persons and objects not directly in evidence, though furnished as well as possible by the imagination; and besides, they are "verbal" images, which is to say that the words give us exactly the meanings and makings for the language of poetry.

But though *Verbal Icon* stands in the title of Mr. Wimsatt's book, there is a profusion of varied chapters; and one of them for our special notice is called "The Concrete Universal." To the best of my knowledge the phrase was coined by Georg Wilhelm Friedrich Hegel (1770–1831), who was doubtless the principal German philosopher of the 18th and 19th centuries after Immanuel Kant (1724–1804). I think we hesitate to employ so stubborn a phrase in which two terms radically opposed must continue leaning upon each other till they fall hopelessly apart. But it was a pet usage for its designer, inasmuch as Hegel was enamored on principle with the linkage of opposites. We observe that "concrete" means "individual" or "particular," while "universal" must be equivalent to "an abstract" or "a generalization" or even "a sheer substance." The compounded phrase is not used very often by Hegel, but other philosophers seem to have tried, for his sake and theirs, to make it work naturally and meaningfully. It may be that they have labored rather vainly.

We turn to one of the sections of Hegel's brilliant but formidable *Phenomenology of the Spirit* to study his argument; and first to his "Human Law." He says, "The ethical substance is, thus, in this determination actual concrete substance"; the end words being contradictory. But, presently, "As an actual substance, that spirit is a nation; as a concrete consciousness, it is the citizens of a nation."

And in the paragraph which follows: "In the form of universality, that spirit is law known to everybody, familiar and recognized, and is everyday, present custom; in the form of particularity it is the concrete certainty of itself in any and every individual; and the certainty of itself as a single individuality is that spirit in the form of government."

Then he treats of the "Divine Law." "Over against this power and publicity of the ethical secular human order there appears, however, the divine law. For the ethical power of the state, being the movement of self-conscious action, finds its opposition in the simple immediate essential being of the moral order; as actual concrete universality, it is a force exerted against the independence of the individual; and, as actuality in general, it finds inherent in that essential being something other than the power of the state." Clearly the "something other" is the Divine Law. But only twice, in the first and third of the three paragraphs, does he employ the phrases "actual concrete substance" and "actual concrete universality."

Kant's three great *Critiques* were studied closely by the young Hegel. But the two philosophers took their respective stances with some variances between them. A very conscious religious sense was deeply implanted in both parties, but Kant was less importunate than the bold young Hegel, and would not undertake to be familiar with the unknown God. We may compare the programs of the two, and not without observing the triplicities of their phrases. It was characteristic of Kant to say in one place: "I have found it necessary to deny knowledge of *God, freedom,* and *immortality,* in order to find a place for *faith.*" Hegel deals with his own three pieties more neatly, as "Aesthetic and Religion and Philosophy." But he made what most of us will think is a grave divergence from philosophical propriety: asserting that he knew God and His goodness, though others might not. The defense of his claim was a saying of his own coinage: "Whatever is true is rational, and whatever is rational is true." But his confidence was not catching. The rationality of the transcendent God would seem to be His own well-kept secret; yet on the whole it appears, as our history advances, that we regard the human situation with more and more satisfaction. We are grateful to old Kant for his formulation of Aesthetic; and from Hegel his junior we have Religion in some sense, and of course Philosophy. But the faculty which we have developed to our greatest advantage, and in obedience to our powerful instincts, is surely—Imagination.

And as to the speech that the critic may use. We may say that ordinarily the critic's language, though less immediate than the poet's, should be less reductive than the philosopher's; in order that he may remember, and permit his gentle readers to remember, that the language of poetry is the language of feeling, not the language of epistemology. This may be said without prejudice to the rights both of science and technology; they compose the universal grammar or logic of knowledge, and are seemingly devoid of any feeling except their preoccupation with absolute definition. Philosophy would then be different even from the pursuit of knowledge by the scientists; it would suspend even those feelings in order to bring all the knowledges under the widest possible perspective. The satisfaction destined for the philosopher will be a philosophic satisfaction; the cake which he would bake will be the cake which he will cut. And if the scientist finds it painful to reflect that the love of his special wisdom caused him to abandon certain early emotions, he is like some poor existentialist who wonders if there is any stage of the human panorama to which he may decently return, in order to reclaim his humanity.

It may be said that the notion of the poem as a concretion, but not a universal, must generate more excitement than Episteme. The author of the poem is Spirit residing though partially and intermittently in the poet and, hopefully at least, identical with that Spirit of the universe which is God, or that Spirit of history which continually creates in order to objectify

174

itself. This Spirit is of an order which only concreteness can express. It cannot have its being within the servile restrictions of the technical sciences. The scientific universals are hopelessly abstract, they are mere concepts; and though these mean to hold their ground, it is only to keep what each of them characteristically wants of the world, and to reject more than they take. Quite different are the occasions when the world somewhere seems possessed and sustained through and through by the concretions of the Spirit; for example, when a natural landscape is utterly beautiful, with every feature adapted to the common tone; still better in the more responsive world of human affairs, when there is realized beside some hearth a scene of perfect familial accord; or when a whole people is exalted in a moment of crisis by the consciousness of serving a just State. Coming to the fine arts, and to poetry which he considered the best of them, Hegel found that poems not only are the recapitulations of the Spirit in the act of occupying its world, but are inclined to extend its triumphs even beyond the known and decent limits of actuality. They mean to make us conscious of our own spiritual nature. Hegel's passion is an elevated humanism, if we cling to secular scruple, but its emotion is religious.

But the effects of poetry do not necessarily require of the critic a difficult "philosophy" and a very special learning. In recent years I have fancied a version that is simpler, and indeed it is homely, and practical. Let it be said frankly that a poem is an organism in action. But we must figure what the organs are; and quickly we decide that they are three in number; namely, the head, the heart, and the feet. Each organ has to play a special part, and each must reconcile itself with two other parts until all are in a common agreement. The three of them are harmonizing and vocalizing all at the same time; the poem is a verbal and vocal job. But the vocalism is not like the outpouring of operatic or instrumental music; it is closer to meditative and imaginative prose.

The three organs are related to each other at least as nearly as are the parts of formal music. The head has to be the intellectual organ, and especially attentive to keeping the logical clarity of the text, and the finality of the conclusion. It has as much conscience in this respect as prose has, and is slow to waive its simple purity; for instance if the heart tries its patience by wanting to use words and phrases which are fateful and strange but too rich and rare for the common barbarian reader. But just often enough it is possible to persuade the honest head that a quotidian language will not do for good verse; till the head finally concurs, and is rewarded by receiving some rare intimations of immortality, for which it will be unexpectedly but eternally grateful.

But the give-and-take in the exchanges from organ to organ is often imperfect insofar as the feet—that is, the meters or rhythms, and the rhymes too if they are engaged—do not aspire faithfully to the obligations of reciprocity. That is the weakness of a great deal of meaningful verse in this century, especially among the younger American poets of one or two or three generations ago. But the scholarship in this respect has been much improved by virtue of the instructions freely offered and gratefully received in the academies. Let this be our cheery conclusion.